big city
JUNK

Mary Randolph Carter

Photographs by the Author

Clarkson Potter/Publishers
New York

Published by Clarkson Potter/Publishers, New York, New York.
Member of the Crown Publishing Group.
Random House, Inc. New York, Toronto, London, Sydney, Auckland
www.randomhouse.com

CLARKSON N. POTTER is a trademark and POTTER and colophon are registered trademarks of Random House, Inc.

Printed in China

Design by Tracy Monahan

Library of Congress Cataloging-in-Publication Data
Carter, Mary Randolph.
Big city junk / by Mary Randolph Carter.—1st ed.
Includes index.
1. House furnishings. 2. Secondhand trade. I. Title.
TX315.C36   2001
747—dc21   2001016350

ISBN 0-609-60712-X

10 9 8 7 6 5 4 3 2 1
First Edition

For Carter and Sam,
Survivors of the Big City
and too much Junk

BIG CITY BONUS

MRC's personal junking diaries to the Big Apple (page 34), Miami (page 58), the nation's capital (page 74), San Francisco (page 88), Big "D" (page 114), Boston (page 140), L.A. (page 152), Chicago (page 186), and Atlanta (page 206).

ACKNOWLEDGMENTS

Big City Junk was a true coast-to-coast journey. My biggest thank-you goes to my husband, Howard, who accompanied me on many trips, drove the car, hauled the finds, waited patiently while I snapped the last picture, and endured my pleas to go just a few more miles to find that last great junk spot. My son, Carter, whose first pad away from home was my first project for *Big City Junk* (see page 23), supported me not only by sharing his personal lair, but by leading me through the city I thought I knew to his own junk sources. In the middle of writing *Big City Junk*, my younger son, Sam (never one particularly moved by junk), surprised me when he insisted on keeping a $10 city landscape I had found at the 26th Street Flea Market to decorate his new city apartment.

And now a big city-by-big city thank-you to all who shared their junk, tales, favorite places and people along the way. I'll be back!

in atlanta
Thanks go to my old friend Ben Apfelbaum, who scooped me up at the airport and whizzed me off to the Lakeville Flea Market and all the other right places. And thanks to Nette Gonzales, a junker and dealer who shared lots of her southern resources and welcomed me to her booth at Lakeville.

in boston
Two good Virginia friends helped me make junk connections (thank you, Jim Harrison) and provided a luxurious nest for Howard and me to collapse in at the end of long days (thank you, Royall Turpin). Thanks to two junking brothers—Bobby and Wayne Garrett. Your junk leads were off the beaten track (just ask Howard!) and so inspiring.

in chicago
Even though she was out of town during my Chicago dig, my old college roommate, artist Jeanette Pasin-Sloan, steered me in the right direction. Thank you, Donald Norwicke: though you live in New York, you certainly haven't lost your junking roots in your native city. Thank you, Patrick Ewing and Michael Willard, who guided me to the treasures of junking in their city. Mary Beth Hughes and Fred Schneider have always dreamed the junker's dreams. Thanks and keep the faith!

in dallas
Thank you, Ann Fox, for being my tour guide through Dallas. Your store, Room Service, was one of my first loves. And thank you, Robin Lowery, for squiring me around and risking arrest in the back of Mark's car! That would be Mark Clay, an old buddy from New York, who returned to his home state and made a great home for himself in a hat factory. Thanks, Mark. Ann led me to Kay Chefchis and Portia Maloney—two great junk collectors, whom you shall meet in a future junk book. F.A. and Maury Midlo, thank you from MRC and Howie.

in los angeles
Always at the top of my thank-you list is the Warner-Garrick family—Laurie, Eddie, and Spicey! They led me to their neighbor Bobby Furst and to artist Shari Elf. And to another junk fan who I met for the first time on this journey, Chloe Ross.

in miami

Jennifer Li scripted my tour through Miami Beach and introduced me to the highly disciplined Fred Bernstein, who edited down a house full of junk to one room! Thanks, Jen. And very warm thanks to Patti and Karl Stoecker for sharing their tie-dyed dream house. Tamara Hendershott, thank you for knowing that I had to meet Patti and Karl. How right you were!

in new york city

Thanks again to Carter Berg, a natural-born junker and photographer. Thanks, Luke Siegel, for downtown junk directions. Anita Calero and Don Freeman generously added to the urban junk experience with their very personal environments; thank you both. Artist John Bennett created a whole new genre of urban junk, and Big City Junk is its first exhibit. Thanks, John. And thank you to James de la Vega for sending messages of hope to city dwellers like the one I first discovered on page 10. Christopher Bailey and David Horowitz are on another urban pilgrimage, which you shall share. Thanks, gentlemen! And thank you Lisa Durfee, a junk sister whose collector's eye is always an inspiration.

in san francisco

My friend Tracey Wheeler, an ex-New Yorker, led me to Randy Saunders, Jeremy Blas, and Mike Madrid. My friend Barbara DeWitt led me to Aria, my favorite junker's haven in San Francisco, where I met Bill Haskell. Bill led me to Pamela "Fritzie" Fritz. Allan Davis who owns Yard Art, turns out to be from Richmond, Virginia, my birthplace. My nephew Tom Coates just recently moved to San Francisco; he lives around the corner from Fritzie, and his father went to school with Allan. Junkers are family, too—thank you, one and all!

in washington, d.c.

Big thanks to Annie Groer, whom I first met when she reviewed *Kitchen Junk* for the *Washington Post*. Turns out she is a junker and invited me to review her political junk. Thank you, Michael Sussman, for sharing the great tradition of the Georgetown Flea Market.

Nothing comes to pass in my junk world without my art director and soul-sister, Tracy Monahan. This is our third collaboration in junk, but who's counting? Thanks, T., for all the inspired junk interpretations with images and words! Thank you to my agent, Steve Axelrod; what a journey. This one ended with a new publisher, Clarkson Potter, and a new editor, Annetta Hanna, to whom I owe the largest debt for editing with a sure hand and a warm heart. At Potter, thanks also go to Marysarah Quinn, Caitlin Israel, Mark McCauslin, Joan Denman, and Elizabeth Royles. Susan Stevens, my loyal cohort and friend, thank you for the daily "junk" you put up with (in and out of the books!). Thank you, Ralph Lauren, for twelve years of inspiration and the opportunity to lead more than one life! I dedicated my first junk book to my mother and father, who have always looked beyond appearances for true worth. The lessons and the love grow with the years.

junkfully, Carter

THE PRESSURE OF SURVIVAL IN THE

LOSE SIGHT - OF YOUR DRE

BIG CITY

WILL MAKE YOU LOSE

M...   HANG IN THERE.

- DE LA VEGA

BIG CITY JUNK

Junking has no boundaries. We junk where we can, and when. Being raised in the country, but choosing to seek my fortune in New York, I always denied the big city's influence in my home. I surrounded myself with things of the country—old wooden worktables, rocking chairs, hand-sewn samplers, and candles everywhere. It was my little rebellion. I might get into a cab in the morning, but I could come home at night and rock my children in a big old rocking chair and smell the melting wax of hand-dipped candles. Now some twenty years later, our apartment still hints of that personal rebellion, but it's come a long way. The samplers have been replaced by paintings found on the street, in city thrift shops and flea markets. The old jug lamps with the gingham shades have made room for Chinese figurines retrieved from the city sidewalks and stoop sales. The sofa is layered with African mud cloths invigorating my old collection of ticking and needlepoint throw pillows. It is a more heterogeneous environment, reflective of how our lives have changed, and of my gradual acceptance that I have made a home in the big city.

Left: Signs of big city living in our New York City apartment—from left to right a faux leopard-skin candlestick holder, African mud cloths draped on the arm and back of the sofa, an Elvis pillow brought back from a Hollywood junket, and a New York cityscape picked up for a few bucks from a flea market in lower Manhattan. **Above, from left to right:** A portrait by James de la Vega of his mother paired with a photograph of the portrait, a gift from Carter Berg to his mother; another view of our Big City–accessorized sofa; a desktop exhibit of a black-and-white photograph of me snapping a street mural by James de la Vega in East Harlem resides next to a 1985 Polaroid of Carter, Sam, and me cozily squeezed into the backseat of an Alaskan float plane.

signs of the city: an alphabet soup of salvaged letters strewn on the cement parking lot transformed on weekends into one of New York's finest fleas — the Grand Bazaar on West 25th Street.

junker's picnic: laid out at the Lakewood Antiques Market in Atlanta.

Big City Junk extends the borders of the junking experience by confining it (not limiting it) within the city limits. Though my last three junk books tiptoed into town, almost like an accidental tourist (thank you, Anne Tyler), they quickly retreated to the comforts of country roads and the green acres of flea markets, backyard sales, and funky rural auctions. Perhaps those journeys were slightly idealized, particularly for city dwellers seeking solace and cheap treasures around the next corner of the dirt road. For those of you who have shared *American Junk*, *Garden Junk*, and *Kitchen Junk*, you know I never start a book without some sort of mea culpa— for not being a gardener, a cook, etc. This time I am admitting I do live in the city and, at last, I am not apologizing for it.

office on the move: though most cabbies are used to hauling big loads of groceries, shoppers' splurges, and even large dogs, bringing work home like this might not make it. Consider not the purchase, but how to get it home.

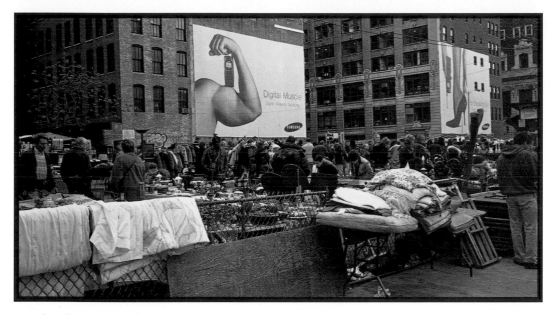

on the fence: at the 26th Street flea market in New York City you can eye the goods over the fence, then decide if you want to pay the $1 entry fee.

junk to go: a VW bus from the Sixties ready to haul away good stuff at the Alemany Flea Market in San Francisco.

sidewalk office: the stool was $10, the phone call 25¢.

Big City Junk boldly embraces the city as the new kingdom of junk. In the last year I have crisscrossed America seeking my junk fortune in New York, Chicago, Boston, San Francisco, Los Angeles, Dallas, Atlanta, Washington, D.C., and Miami. My dream would have been to drive like John Steinbeck in *Travels with Charley* or like Richard Farnsworth on his John Deere tractor mower in *Straight Story*. Limited by time, as we all are, I mostly flew on years of accumulated mileage. Flying also set heavy restrictions on my personal foraging. I learned a certain discipline (an important Big City virtue, as you will see) in editing the size—unfortunately not the number—of my purchases, and made a huge leap in the art of carry-on packing. (See tips on Long-Distance Junking, page 18.) My original list of Big Cities was much longer, but I just plumb ran out of time. So, to all of you junkers whose cities and treasures I missed, be happy that I have left your secret resources unexplored. But hold on, the Big City journey isn't over yet!

Living in the city offers each of us different types of challenges, but there are definitely five that everyone shares: the need for privacy, storage, general living space, as well as home space for work, and a lot more discipline. If you are a junker, and I presume that you are, then each of these, and especially discipline, is far more challenging for you than for the normal person. Not to worry, you are about to meet some very ingenious junkers who have confronted at least one, if not all five, of the ferocious Big City challenges! They have even figured out, I'm happy to report, how to overcome or compensate with the secret delight of our daily lives—more JUNK!

Privacy

We all have ways of creating our own private space. Sometimes it's just the allusion of privacy, like the crimson sarong tied up over the door to Patti and Karl Stoecker's Miami Beach bedroom. (See page 56.)

- As evening falls, Don Freeman slides a 14-foot-long canvas curtain across a ceiling track to create a cozy sleeping nook in his wide-open living space in New York City. (See page 94 for his "now you see it, now you don't" bedroom.

- Old wooden shutters have been our shield against prying eyes and New York City lights. (Take a look on page 42.) In downtown Dallas, Mark Clay built a cozy sleeping loft in the converted hat factory he lives in, so he wouldn't have to cover his windows.

Discipline

Mark Clay has it. He even uses plastic IVs to precisely nourish his orchids while he's away (see page 113). Anita Calero also has discipline. She collects small things, like shells, ribbon, and matchboxes (see page 199), and keeps them organized in little, neatly labeled boxes hidden away in a large cabinet (see page 201) until she wishes to view them. Fred Bernstein, the man who emptied a huge house and moved into something like a motel room (see page 189) on the beach, certainly has it! Discipline is the virtue junkers probably don't have enough of. It's one to seriously cultivate, especially if you live in the city. You don't have enough space, you never have enough money, your closets are a war zone, and you do a lot of work at home. What this all means is that you need to think a little harder about what you buy and where you're going to put it. Or if you must continue to hoard, consider a stoop sale to depossess yourself of the old stuff and make room for the new old stuff.

Storage

There's never enough. Even without all the stuff!

- Randy Saunders and Jereny Blas turned a long, skinny closet in their San Francisco apartment into a one-person computer-using and bill-paying space. The problem, then, was where to hang their coats and store their luggage. The solution: a pair of tall, skinny school lockers. (See page 81.)

- Mark Clay stacked together a dozen industrial storage drawers to file away his shorts, T-shirts, belts, and architectural drawings. He identified each drawer with a Magic Markered luggage tag to save on guessing time. (See pages 108–109.)

- Anita Calero lives in a spacious loft with hundreds of tiny collections. They're out of sight, which is the way she likes them. (See page 199.)

16

I don't know how it happened, but the apartment we lived in with our two sons for more than twenty-five years somehow enlarged. Not physically (I'm not that crazy yet), but emotionally. Over the years the four of us found ways to share and expand walls, shelves, and closets. It helped when the boys moved out, and yet I still have this fantasy about renting my own storage space. There are warehouses all over the city committed to containing urban overflow. I visited a few and then decided to create my own—rent free. It's not available at the moment, but feel free to check it out on page 131.

Whether you live on two floors of a town house in San Francisco like Pamela "Fritzie" Fritz on page 160, or in a studio in Manhattan, like Carter Berg's (seen above), or in the equivalent of a motel room in Miami Beach, as Fred Bernstein does, it's home sweet home, and to each his or her own. Fritzie, Carter, and Fred have nothing in common except that they've successfully figured out how to live with their large collections in given amounts of space.

Whether we work in an office or our office is a cell phone and a car, or a warehouse under a bridge, or a laptop on a plane, most of us bring work home. Homework can also be printing photos, writing a book, recycling junk into art, or tie-dyeing vintage slips. Whatever it is, the real work is finding space. For Carter Berg, it's a table (see page 27); for Randy Saunders, it's a closet (above, see more on page 84); for Shari Elf, it's a shack in her tiny Los Angeles backyard (see page 118); and for Fritzie Fritz, it's a cozy white studio on the top floor of her town house (see page 172). Some workers need personal clutter, others need total order. All of us thrive in a stress-free personal environment called home.

FUN!

Oh, and by the way, city life is also fun, filled with romance, adventure, money, and success. Don't get the wrong idea from all the storage problems and the discipline issues. Every story in this book has a happy ending. (Sing it, Frank! "If I can junk it there . . . I can junk it anywhere . . . ")

the street

It's all out there. Just find out when the official Big Trash Day is in your city. People throw out the darnedest things. Of course, you don't have to wait. There are treasures abandoned on the street all the time. One of my favorites is this child's painting that I found on a trash can, in front of a school in our neighborhood.

the yard

No, we're not talking Scotland Yard, but the local recycling yard! Shari Elf (see page 128) pays regular visits to hers, not only to drop stuff off, but to hunt for treasure. Not all yards allow this, so check out the guidelines. Most recycling yards (aka dumps, when I was growing up) have designated days for claiming other people's throwaways that become your treasures.

the alley

You'll never spot Shari Elf's car on the main thoroughfares of L.A. She takes the alleys—less traffic and lots of interesting junk. Her newest challenge? Those big PVC trash containers! Nonetheless, Shari finds plenty of treasures and then recycles them into her artwork. (See my portrait on page 9.)

off the beaten path

Big cities are a melting pot of multiple cultures. The Chinatowns of San Francisco, Los Angeles, and New York offer an entirely alternative shopping experience. Not only is there great souvenir junk, but there are also really nice, inexpensive handmade objects. One of my favorite stores is Pearl River Trading Company in New York City's Chinatown. You can find a whole array of beautiful paper lanterns (like the one seen in Patti Stoecker's dining room, on page 51). Little Havana in Miami is another great experience. (See page 58, for more.) And don't forget to stay for lunch or dinner!

the web

Though cyberjunking will never replace the experience of digging through a box of stuff, it does offer some advantages, as well as a community of friendly and helpful on-line junkers. A personal tale: I bid on-line on a wonderful light-boxed portrait of a little ballerina (see above). I lose. I e-mail the winning bidder and explain how I am working on a book called *Big City Junk* and want to include the ballerina in a special chapter. After some funny back-and-forth e-mails, he informs me, "You win," and e-mails the seller to relinquish his claim. In the meantime, I've dropped that chapter from this volume, but I wanted to thank my new on-line friend—Mark Saunders from Sacramento, California — for giving in to a needy junker.

city thrift

There are nearly 100 thrift shops in New York. (And as many or more in all big cities.) Most of them are set up to benefit charities. When you buy there, you're not only fulfilling your junker's cause, but someone else's.

carry-on junk

You've decided to take in the junking at the Lakewood Antiques Market in Atlanta. You fly in, rent a car, and spend a day foraging for southern gold. Halfway through, bags loaded, you stop for a barbeque, and think, "Wait a minute, how in the heck am I getting all this stuff back?" This can't happen—you've got to have a packing strategy before you leave home. Your options:

1. Drive home.

2. Shop with discipline. (Remember? If not, see page 16.) Focus on small, nonbreakable items. Travel with bubble wrap, or ask the dealer if he/she can wrap your items carefully. I always travel with one or two extra nylon duffels to transport extra junk home. Normally, I carry my loot on to the plane with me and stow it in the overhead compartment. If things are packed really well, you can check them. You just don't want to incur overweight charges and blow those bargains!

3. Have it sent. Luckily, when I traveled to Atlanta, my friend and sympathetic junker Ben Apfelbaum helped me out by UPSing whatever I couldn't fit into my carry-ons. You can do that yourself, if you can manage to find the boxes, tape, etc. If you're staying in a hotel, ask the concierge to assist you. When I purchased a large painting of Chicago at Brooke James Ltd. (see page 187), the owners, Lisa and Keri Brennan, had it carefully shipped to me at no charge. Junkers are the nicest, most helpful people.

junk love: never too late

Some of us are born to junk. We start hoarding and collecting before we even know what we're doing. It wasn't like that for Patti Stoecker. Her calling came late, after a successful modeling career, falling in love with her husband Karl, birthing two baby girls, and moving with all of them to a wreck of an old house in Miami Beach. (See the whole story on page 46.) Her first week there she walked into Debris, the perfect place for a junker to be born. And there it was— a boudoir chair in crushed velvet with a heart-shaped back. It was $25, and love at first sight! That's how it begins, so innocently, with one silly chair. And then the craving sets in for just one more . . . and one more. Oh, junker's love— unquenchable and awesome!

questions not to ask yourself

Do I need this?
Do I have a place for this?
Do I have one already?

to haggle or not to haggle

This is not the question! It's part of the sport. Dealers expect it. But they also love their stuff, so don't insult them by throwing out a ridiculously low price. If something's marked $35, offer $20—you might get it for $26. In pricing their goods, most dealers factor in a cushion of 5 to 20 percent, so when you ask, "Can you do any better?" that's normally the figure they'll quote. But not always. Variables that could affect their answer include how long they've had the object, how much they have invested in it, and what time of day it is.

junk casual

Forget the fact that you're in the city. If you're junking, you dress for junking, no matter where you are. My flea market uniform consists of a loose cotton shirt, cargo pants with good pockets, sneakers or boots (depending upon the season), my junker's vest, and an old, weathered sea captain's cap. The vest takes the place of a backpack or pocketbook. It's a portable file cabinet for storing checks, cash, ID, a small magnifying glass for taking a closer look at the merchandise, sun lotion, a Swiss army knife, disposable towelettes, and a list of what you're searching for —the junker's compass.

transportation

taxis
Getting the stuff home is always the challenge, particularly when you're in the middle of a big city. Taxis can really accommodate a lot of stuff, as long as the driver's willing and his trunk is not filled with his own junk.

buses
City buses, and subways too, are easy cheap transportation to a junker's destination. Why spend the money on getting there? Save it to splurge on the way home. If you're hauling a big load, wait for an emptier bus and head all the way to the back.

hoofing it
There's no better way to connect with a city than to walk its streets. In Chicago, for example, there are neighborhoods loaded with collector's haunts. Take a cab or bus to get there, then get out and walk. Carrying your loot is the main drawback.

rental cars
In many cities, like Boston, for example, the junking spots are spread all over the city. If you feel comfortable driving, there's nothing like having the luxury of all that portable space. Downside: finding a place to park.

a driver
When I junk in the city, particulary a city I am not familiar with, I always try to get a friend or a friend of a friend to drive me around. If you're absolutely on your own and have limited time, you might want to splurge and pay for a car and driver.

a friend
Going for an out-of-town junk jaunt? Call ahead and book a friend. While they're chauffeuring, you can concentrate on where you want to go, and stay on track. I always offer to pay for gas and lunch, and I try to find some little junker's treat to reward them with.

junk reporte

Take a little camera—it can be a disposable, point-and-shoot, or Polaroid—to record the catch you've just landed. I prefer taking instant pictures and writing the price and the dealer right on the frame of the picture. When I go home I enter into a notebook the picture, the price, comments on its condition, the card from the dealer (if available), and the receipt. My decade's worth of junk journals is ready to be stored in my ministorage unit (see page 137).

schlepping

I gave up carrying a purse to flea markets ages ago. As mentioned above, I wear my fishing vest, and carry my camera in a little canvas army bag. As for hauling around the booty at a flea market, I prefer to take a couple of Mexican nylon shopping bags. Craft Caravan in New York City is my personal source for these indispensable accessories. (See the Junk Guide, page 232.) The really accommodating flea markets actually have wagons to help you transport unwieldy stuff. Dealers are also very nice about letting you leave big stuff to pick up later. (Just don't forget where you left it.) And check out the urban transportation an enterprising street person came up with, below.

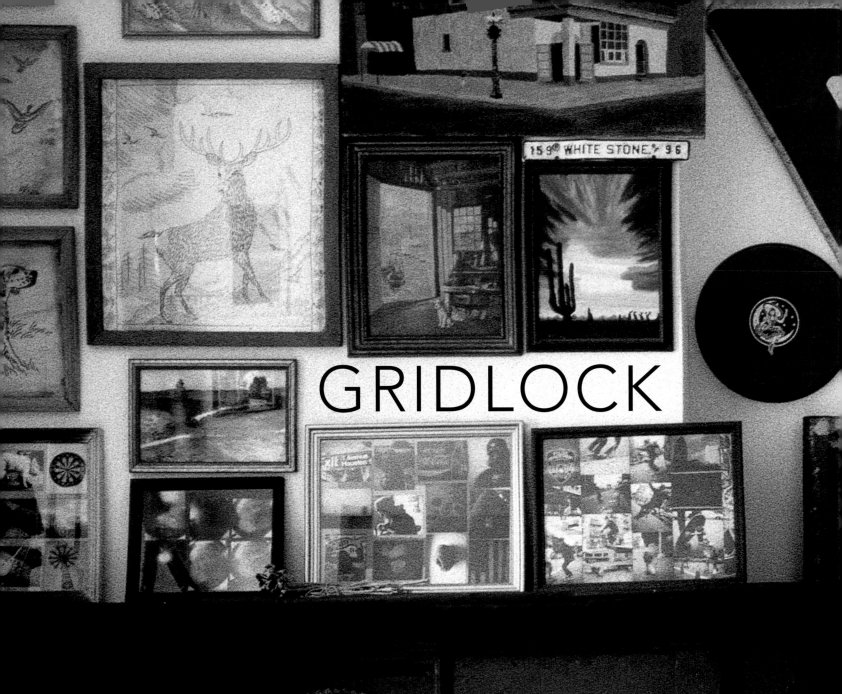

GRIDLOCK

Right and preceding pages: The first thing Carter Berg dragged up the stairs to his new downtown digs was an old mantelpiece generously donated by his mother. It anchors his big city collection of art and objects gathered from junking and photo expeditions in the city and around the world. The YIELD sign was spotted abandoned under the Manhattan Bridge. The green gate from an old Ford pickup was a housewarming present from his good friend Luke Siegel, who hauled it back from a junkyard in Maine. The drum to the left of it is like the ones played by the West African drummers in Central Park. He custom-ordered it for $250. The Edward Hopperish-looking painting of a city street, in the upper left corner, was his first investment in his new home. He discovered it in the East Village at Repeat Performance for only $20. He created his first Polaroid montage, like the one seen above the yellow MERGE sign and on the far right corner of the mantel, four years ago as a last-minute gift for a friend. They are his handcrafted short stories of life and junk in his big city hometown.

When Carter Berg digs for signs to add to his traffic gallery, seen opposite, he takes a walk to the SoHo flea market, where he picked up the FALLOUT SHELTER sign, seen above and left, for $12.

Until a year and a half ago, Carter Berg shared a room with his brother Sam in an apartment building twelve stories high on the East Side of New York City. Actually, the room had been partitioned when he was ten and Sam was six, so they each had their own space. Carter's measured about 10 by 15 feet. There for about twenty years, he created a very big world in what many people would consider a box. He never felt limited, but found a creative way to use every inch of floor and wall. When he moved (and note I didn't say "finally moved," because I am his mother and would have been happy to have him stay forever) into a studio apartment measuring 24 by 16 feet, he applied all the space-saving principles learned in those early, cozy years. On the south wall, seen at left and on the preceding pages, is his traffic gallery of city street signs, as well as signs of city life captured in flea market paintings, license plates, and a collection of his own Polaroid montages. There are a Keith Haring skateboard, a gate from the back of an old pickup, a customized African drum, a fire alarm box from Massachusetts, souvenirs from his neighborhood on the fringes of Chinatown, old paintbrushes hung like 3-D Jim Dines, a worktable (see page 27) laid out like a mini-exhibit, new and old cameras everywhere, and his prized GLOBE CANVAS bike messenger sign that he pried off the building (with permission from the owners) after they went out of business. He has stretched the restrictions of studio living, turning the physical area into a very large personal space filled with the collected treasures of his big city life—from childhood to now.

Above: Carter's studio is actually L-shaped. The entrance, where the kitchen is also tucked away, is located at the tip of the L, to the right of his walk-in closet, seen at the lower right of this wide-angle view. Taking a dog nap in his very patriotic sleeping alcove are Carter and Charley, his black Lab and most cherished treasure.

Opposite, clockwise from top left: 1. Perfect to wheel around the apartment, an old metal typewriter table supports bedside music, reading glasses, and artwork. The standing brass-shaded lamp, another gift from Mom, sheds some light on two of Carter's adolescent passions—skateboarding and the art of Keith Haring. The skateboard, from The Pop Shop, located in New York City's SoHo section, was his own special pick for his twelfth birthday. The DETOUR sign was found at a flea market in upstate New York for $10. **2.** What a journey this (very heavy) cast-iron fire alarm box has taken. It hails originally from Newton, Massachusetts, circa 1950. Carter's aunt Nell (my sister) found it in a junk shop on the Outer Banks of North Carolina. She dragged it to American Junk, our former junk store in White Stone, Virginia, where Carter spotted it, bought it for $50, and then trucked it back to our farm in upstate New York. It lived there until he brought it down to his new home in New York City's Little Italy, and heaved it up the stairs to its final (he hopes) resting place. A couple of stuffed polar bears Polaroided at the Museum of Natural History, and now part of another Carter montage, hang above it. Below them and to the left of the firebox is a small hubcap from the SoHo flea market. **3.** Charley in his place of honor surrounded by less animate pets—a bunny from Carter's grandmother Pat, and a sleeping leopard, a gift at his birth. The tattered American flag has followed him from home to college to here. The other flag, not in much better shape, hails from an auction a million summers ago in Nags Head, North Carolina; it was one of six the family divided up for $10 each. **4.** The flag's stripe of yellow inspired Carter to paint the same color at the foot of the bed. The Sixties triple-swivel floor lamp was left behind by the last tenant. The Polaroid montage of the Williamsburg Bridge is one of Carter's. **5.** From Carter's favorite neighborhood store on Mott Street, Pearl River, comes this $2 Chinese poster.

24

Carter's vintage Rolleiflex camera is the fitting centerpiece for the mini-exhibition of favorite finds and souvenirs he has laid out so carefully on top of his country worktable. It's a sturdy monument to a picture-taking passion that has sent him roving the streets of New York and around the world, clicking his own pictures and assisting more established photographers. It has also fueled his hunt for every sort of camera, three of which are displayed here. The two in the back right, seen in greater detail on the next page, were in disrepair when he bought them for $5 and $10 respectively. He may have them repaired one day, but in the meantime he enjoys the look of them. Another beacon worth noting is the black-and-white-swirled Cape Hatteras lighthouse replica towering over everything from the back window. It was a summer birthday present, and stands as a reminder of family summers on the Outer Banks of North Carolina. Bookending the table are, on the far left, a trio of old paintbrushes over a sign that spells out EASY LOADER, and on the far right a hot plate souvenir of Little Italy bought at another neighborhood store on Mulberry Street.

Left: The support for this incredible show of minutiae comes from an old scrubbed oak table Carter picked up during his college days in the far reaches of northwestern New York State. It cost about $25 and has removable legs—well suited to his peripatetic life.

Clockwise from top left: 1. A handpainted lampshade for CLB by Nick Gamarello. The lamp base is an old candle mold. **2.** From left to right, a patch from the original New York City messenger bag company, Globe Canvas. An El Pico coffee can stores his frame brushes. A vintage bottle of Carter's ink, $5, plucked from a crowded table at the Grand Bazaar flea market on West 25th Street. Our Lady of Guadalupe (Carter and I have adopted her as the patron saint of junkers) imprinted on a tall glass votive candle jar, found at a local grocery store for a couple of dollars. A chunk of petrified wood from a shoot in Moab, Utah. **3.** This set of dominoes, with unclassic colored dots, was 50¢ at the Garage on West 25th Street, New York City. **4.** The gold pocket watch from a pawnshop in Moab, Utah, has a special college graduation message engraved on the back from Mom and Dad. (Who says you can't gift-shop in the wacky malls of junk?) The quartet of rocks are another Carter shoot souvenir from Moab. **5.** A color Xerox of a Polaroid of big city souvenirs outlined in corrugated cardboard. **6.** A bird's-eye view of the dominoes seen above, surrounded by more dominoes; a Zippo lighter from a gas station; a U.S. Department of Agriculture and Forest Service belt buckle from a thrift shop in Palm Desert, California; an old-fashioned bottle opener with a red wooden handle; and to the lower far left, a beaded cigarette case, $4 at The Green Flea on Saturdays at East 67th Street and York Avenue. **7.** Clockwise from top left, a Lady of Guadalupe medal, $3, from an East Village shop; a box of wooden matches from a trip to Jamaica; a Saint Bernard medal; the lens cap for Carter's Rolleiflex; and a push-pin pile. **8.** A magazine portrait of the Belgian model Tanga Moreau by friend and photographer Bruce Weber and a duo of used cameras—an 8mm movie camera and a Polaroid Land camera—picked up at junk shops for $5 and $10 respectively. **9.** A fringe of black-and-white and color Polaroids. **10.** Sunbaked antlers from Whitefish, Montana, hold Carter's simple silver rings. The trio of lightning bolts (his trademark) were hammered out of metal by his friend Luke Siegel. The knife below them was another gift—from Sheila Metzner, a photographer and friend—while on a shoot in Argentina.

From the moment he discovered that the DeMartini Globe Canvas Company, the makers of the original New York City messenger bag, was going out of business and that their factory was just a couple of blocks from his new home, Carter Berg had a mission. He wanted the GLOBE CANVAS sign nailed on the wall next to their entrance. He kept a close eye on the building and finally, after months, it paid off. One day, walking by the factory, he saw signs of life! He went down the stairs to the sub-sidewalk entrance and introduced himself to Mr. DeMartini himself. He explained his wish and within minutes it was granted. A few days later he and a friend pried off the sign and carried it home. Finding the right spot for it took some consideration. Finally, he cleared the studio's north wall and painted it a burnt umber. The sign hangs over his blue Formica-topped kitchen table (the blues work together, he thinks). To the right of it hangs an original black-and-white print by the artist George Groz, made in 1932, a graduation present from some good friends. To him, the sign and the print are equally valuable, which is why junkers are so smart and so stupid at the same time—they're curators of the heart.

Right: The blue Formica-topped table, found at a barn sale in upstate New York for about $20, is kept bare, unlike its wooden counterpart, seen previously. Carter uses it for his favorite morning warmup, a lone cup of coffee and the *New York Times,* as well as a place to serve his favorite pasta to drop-in dinner guests.

When the Globe Canvas masterpiece, seen opposite, was hung, down came the Keith Haring poster and two junk paintings of waterscapes—one of a lake in Maine, at left, and one of a canal in Venice, next to it. Carter just left them propped against the wall for lack of any better space, but then decided he liked the way they looked resting on the sun-splashed bare hardwood floors. Looking around our apartment many blocks uptown, I see I have accommodated an overflow of junk in the same manner. (See one of my dog masterpieces poised on the living room floor on page 44.) Leaning a work against the wall is a good solution for paintings that are very heavy, or that you're not sure about, or when wall space is at a premium.

31

By now you've guessed that my son Carter is a junker like his mom. One of the things he's clearly fascinated with is urban junk, and a subspecies of that category, transportation junk. You have to laugh that even with all the traffic signs (his walls are a testament to the variety) and more and more traffic cops, gridlock, that frustrating tie-up of vehicles all honking at once in an intersection, still tends to be the norm in the big city.

Above: The rattan sofa, $10 at an upstate New York tag sale and covered with an India print spread, is normally taken up by the stretched-out form of a long black dog—Charley. Today it's loaded with assorted camera bags and one yellow counterfeit messenger bag.

Left: Near the entrance of his apartment is Carter's "junk" bike, bought used for $50 at a 14th Street bike store. The security chain hangs over its bars like an oversized bracelet. The army bag, available at most army navy stores for about $20, holds his valuable shooting ammo—Polaroid film. Behind it is an old Bell & Howell camera bag, picked up at the SoHo flea market for $2.

Opposite: The ultimate city junk: the familiar Yellow taxicab sign signaling on or off duty. I found this one at a favorite dealer's booth at, of all places, The Garage, a converted garage space on 25th Street between Sixth and Seventh Avenues. The dealer was Janet West, the price $35—not much more than a cab ride to Kennedy airport.

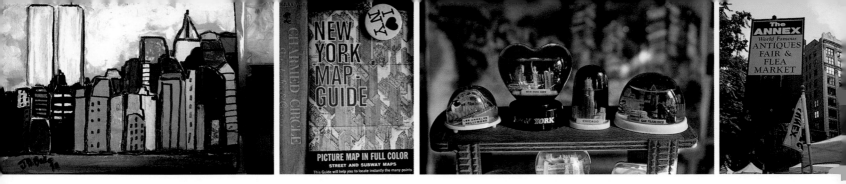

A 3-D cardboard Manhattan skyline picked out of a sidewalk art exhibit on lower Fifth Avenue for $25.

Big Apple memorabilia: map and button.

An instant collection of Big City snow domes—ten in total—discovered on an eBay auction, $50.

N.Y. City's legendary 26th St. flea.

Circa 1950s coloring book.

There are over 100 thrift shops in Manhattan alone!

Office supply out in the open at the Grand Bazaar. I bought the stool in the foreground for $15.

Junker's chic at one of the 26th Street markets.

I loved the display card and all 18

Last-chance souvenirs of the city at the airport gift shop: the Statue of Liberty in rainbow plastics.

The Empire State Building for real!

At Repeat Performance, Big City junk at retail.

The fashion capital of the world presents a Big City parade of vintage Barbies: $2 each.

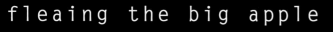

fleaing the big apple

New York, New York — the capital of junkdom. You can hunt through thrift shops, junk shops, flea markets,

Car art on
exhibit on a
SoHo street.

A sidewalk beauty pageant promoting
wigs of all colors on the streets of
New York.

A warning to warm
a junker's heart
at G & S Designs.

A blur of traffic streaks by a
Manhattan skyline in this $5 oil from
the Grand Bazaar on West 25th St.

Toy watches
for $30 at
The Garage.

A vintage traf-
fic light at The
Annex, for $150.

Junk masterpieces on the streets of SoHo.
I picked up my Manhattan skyline, top row
left, at one like this.

Souvenir pillow:
"Wonder City of
the World."

Schoolyards:
weekend
fleas.

Ugly
Luggage,
Brooklyn.

Handcrafted
masks on
Madison Ave.

It's everywhere: Northside Junk is in the
Williamsburg section of Brooklyn, and
not far from Ugly Luggage.

A fashion diva
with fancy acces-
sories. $1.

Graffiti
backdrop
for NYC junk.

sidewalk sales, and streets paved with junker's gold! If you can junk it there, you can
junk it anywhere!

FIFIS ON FIFTH

Small dogs (aka Fifis) rule the city. They were made for sidewalk strutting alongside their fashionable owners, wearing designer collars and leashes. Sometimes you can spot them in packs of eight or more (see a perky pack paused on a New York City curb on the preceding pages) led by a hired dog walker who leads them fearlessly through frenetic crowds, past taunting schoolchildren and noisy construction sites. They look great sitting in limousines and private jets. They fit nicely into crowded elevators and accessorize the best penthouse apartments. The Queen of the Fifis is, of course, the poodle, which is why this chapter is so full of them. They also populate every flea market and tag sale table. They are the junker's best of show.

Clockwise from top left: 1. A ghostly silhouette of a mysterious Fifi strides along the side of a vending machine for the venerable *New York Times*. These street-art pets are a familiar sight on the sidewalks of New York City; they are the bowwow work of street artist Peter Mayer. **2.** Turn back to the previous pages for a big picture of the pet pack shown here. Left to right: The little rope pooch stretched out here and in picture number 8 on the following page was picked up for $1 at one of my friend Lisa Durfee's summer yard sales (To check out her on-line yard sales on eBay, see the Junk Guide, page 233.) The black plastic poodle bank (seen again in picture number 8) was nabbed at a schoolyard flea market in New York City, for $2. His cement pal, picked up at the same flea market, cost twice as much, but weighs twenty times more. I loved his colorful coat. The little porcelain pup between them was a 50¢ investment at a sidewalk sale in New York City's SoHo. The cardboard bulldog was picked off a $5 table at the SoHo flea market. A fancy ceramic poodle curled out of strands of wet clay was part of the French poodle frenzy from the Forties through the early Sixties; I discovered it at the SoHo flea market on West Broadway. Crocheted and knitted poodles were a crafter's craze starting in the Fifties, resulting in a million of these canine camouflages for all-sized bottles and toilet paper rolls. **3.** A flesh-and-blood Fifi struts her stuff! **4.** Pet peeve for building owners, more dog art by Peter Mayer. **5.** A vintage wirehaired fox terrier toy ($45 at The Garage, in New York City) pauses to consider a city gardener's plea. **6.** A classy little toy Scottie (bought years ago for maybe $40) encounters the real thing, a Lab named Charley, in Central Park. **7.** Canine graffiti dogs patrol a city construction site. **8.** This seaworthy pup, perhaps knotted by a sailor, was found on dry land in Lisa Durfee's on-line tag sale on eBay. **9.** A Park Avenue poodle takes a breather on a dainty hand towel offered for $5 by a dealer at the 26th Street flea market, New York City. **10.** A bright red construction wall becomes the temporary canvas for one more big city/little graffiti Fifi.

39

Above and right: Poised outside his fancy city domain, and on the grassy median in the center of New York City's Park Avenue, this plaster poodle was retrieved from a street fair not many blocks away for $1. Made from a plaster mold and originally sold unpainted, there are a million versions of this fetching pooch ready for city or country life!

It wasn't long after World War II, with our American soldiers returning from France, that the whole nation started a love affair with all things French. The mascot then was unquestionably the chic little French poodle. But the famous poodle cut wasn't created by French hairdressers. German hunters who had discovered the dogs' prowess as waterfowl retrievers left fur pompoms around their joints and on their chests to keep them from getting rheumatism from the cold water. The Fifi of all Fifis would go on to become the decorative icon for everything from circle skirts to laundry hampers, and its image would be reproduced a million times as the ceramic Beanie Baby of its time.

It was one of those perfect golden Sunday afternoons in October. Why were we in the city when normally we would have been at our get-away-from-it-all retreat in upstate New York? We were working on *Big City Junk,* of course. I had been shooting some of the city dogs (Fifis!) for this chapter when Howard suggested we take Charley, Carter's black Lab, for a walk in Central Park. We had started out the door to the elevator when I ran back and grabbed Barkham, the little plastic basset hound, seen struggling at left. In the park, I set him up at the base of one of the old water fountains. He looked sadder than ever, struggling to reach the water. A young boy came running up with his father in tow. "Can I help him?" he pleaded? "Of course," I replied. He strode right up and on tiptoes got Barkham's little dry mouth up to the spigot. "Dad, you've got to help!" he implored his father. Dad pushed, the water streamed out, and Barkham had a drink and a bath! After a little conversation with Barkham's new friend and his dad, it was decided that our old basset hound would have a new home. As they left the park, the little boy turned him back toward us. Barkham's sad eyes weren't sad anymore.

Left: Our plastic basset hound, actually a toy bank, struggles for a drink in New York City's Central Park. I fetched him home from the Georgetown flea market in Washington, D.C., for $5 and a dog biscuit!

41

Above: A corner view of our living room—every inch spoken for! The space is dominated by a handmade tin chandelier that we all hit our heads on, a lanky bookshelf crowned with a sailboat from a summer on the Outer Banks of North Carolina, and a weathered Christmas tree shutter, home to a pair of 9 by 12-inch paint-by-number poodle portraits retrieved from The Garage in New York City, for $40.

Right: A close-up of the poodle portraits tacked on to one of the three pairs of beat-up shutters I paid $10 apiece for at the annual Memorial Day tag sale at the Copake auction house, Copake, New York.

Opposite: Though she is only 8 inches tall, don't doubt the fashion authority of Queen Poodle, the editor of *Dogue* magazine. Dressed in red leather from head to paw, she gets her red fuzzy fur permed at Le Chien, the chicest salon in New York City. She was discovered at the Lincoln Road flea market in Miami Beach for $5. Her throne is cushioned by a pink satin souvenir pillow with an image of the nation's capital on the other side. (See one similar on page 35.) These can be hunted down for about $20.

I grew up with big dogs—Saint Bernards—and all of their big dog friends—German shepherds, Labradors, golden retrievers, collies, boxers, dalmatians, and even a Great Dane or two. Until I moved to New York City, many years later, I had no exposure to the world of Fifis. But I never was a Fifi hater. In fact, after I met and married my husband, Howard, I gave him a miniature apricot poodle named Baja to befriend the little blind Yorkshire terrier, Tutu, that he had had for years. After the dogs came the babies, two sons, Carter and Sam. When they were fourteen and eleven (Baja and Tutu having long since gone to Dog Heaven), it was time for Bo, a spirited wirehaired fox terrier. When the boys returned from college, Carter brought Charley, the black (mostly) Lab he had adopted from a local family. We have all lived together—Mom and Dad, boys and dogs—in the same apartment, twelve stories up in New York City, since the boys were born. There are dog hairs on the furniture, paw scratches on the doors, and a rip or two in the furniture from when it thundered and Bo went crazy. Besides the dogs and the dog things—toys, rag pulls, bones, food bowls, unused dog beds (because they prefer ours)— there is the dog decor. There is a fox terrier doorstop at the bedroom door, a little painting of a fox terrier and a Scottie, a yellow poodle lamp, seen on the desk on the opposite page, photos of our dogs everywhere, and weird doggy things like the paint-by-number poodle paintings seen in our living room, opposite, and the cocky little red leather poodle enthroned in its own lap of luxury in our library, seen at left.

43

The model dog walker, at left, excavated from a box of paintings under a table at New York's Grand Bazaar flea market on 25th Street between Fifth and Sixth Avenues, took my junker's breath away. I loved it instantly and probably would have paid much more than the $15 the dealer asked for. I don't think I even haggled over it! What I found so remarkable was not only the subject matter, a woman walking her dog obviously in the city, but the way she was styled. I saw her as a wonderful cross between Jacqueline Kennedy Onassis (the little shift dress more than the hat) and Audrey Hepburn in *Breakfast at Tiffany's* (though she had a cat, not a dog). There is no date on the painting, only the artist's last name —Klages—but it had to have been done in the Sixties. The little dog that she leads is difficult to recognize. Not exactly a poodle, is it perhaps the artist's version of a Bedlington terrier? The painting hangs in my office at Polo Ralph Lauren—a perfect spot for it, don't you think?

Opposite: My eye was caught by this needlepoint portrait of a dear cocker spaniel that was sitting at attention on the blacktop of the SoHo flea market, a transformed parking lot in New York City. A message scrawled in pencil on the back reveals it was more than likely a present to two young brothers—Sammy and Bob—with love from their Aunt Minnie and Nana. It was framed (more clues on the back) in "N. Miami Beach." My guess would be Minnie and Nana retired there from New York and one or both of them hand-stitched this representation of the boys' favorite dog. He now sits patiently in our New York apartment under my desk, next to a school stool I picked up the same day for the same price—$10!

TIE-DYED
& GONE TO HEAVEN

I t was after the eighteenth snowstorm of the winter of 1994 that Patti and Karl Stoecker decided it was time to move out of New York City. They had two small daughters—Sheena, four, and Sami, two—and Karl's son Luke, who was eighteen. They lived for their vacations at the beach and often wondered why they didn't stay there year round. They had bought a wreck of a house in Miami Beach in 1992, thinking one day they would fix it up; now was the time. Patti's not sure why they decided to reside there during the reconstruction, but that's what they did, camping out for six months. After the floors were in and the walls were replastered, her instinct was to paint them white. "But somehow I felt living with white was over." (They had had white walls in their city loft.) It also seemed that white would only point out the house's imperfections. Six years later, the walls are painted pink, grassy green, crimson, and teal blue— not that different from the colors of the vintage slips that Patti tie-dyes and sells, seen on the preceding pages. Her customers tell her they feel so free and happy in them. Which is also how Patti and her family feel in their tie-dyed house.

Left: This was the first vision I had of Patti and Karl's 1929 jewel, with Puppy and Zoe asleep on the cool stone and marble floors. The four matching chairs, about $30 each from a girlfriend's yard sale, were Patti's first purchase in Miami. The cast-iron garden chair at the right end was $5, from the Lincoln Road Flea Market. She got the bentwood chair just behind it, along with a little matching table, for $10 at a boutique in South Beach. The old wooden chandelier came from Victoria's Armoire in Coral Gables and was $100. The nude—a study painted in the Twenties—was brought back from a trip to their favorite shop, Blackwatch, on Metropolitan Avenue in Forest Hills, New York.

Above: Along with the iridescent sheers she discovered at Vintage Soul, Patti added a pair of curtains she ordered from the Anthropologie catalog. These have a golden embossed border that contrasts nicely, but, she confesses, the pairing was totally accidental. "I opened the box and instead of putting them on a shelf (never to be seen again) I draped them over the curtain rods like a display."

Right: Karl found the tulip lamps at a flea market in Fort Lauderdale, Florida, but they had been dunked in baby blue paint. He scraped away a little of the paint and saw some red glass. After paying $10 for each he went home and spent two nights with Q-Tips and paint thinner (and a lot of faith!) in order to restore them to what you see now. The thick yellow glass hanging lamp, seen reflected in the mirror, is a bohemian Spanish piece that Patti bought for $70 from her friend Jean Marie, the owner of Fly Boutique—another favorite store and a source for her slips. The mirror, which was just a frame and not white when she got it, was $18, another Fly Boutique grab.

The stained-glass art project seen on the window ledge, opposite, was made from a kit given to Sheena last Christmas. The presence of both children is strongly felt throughout their home. They, not Mommy, are choosing the new colors for their bedrooms. When they create something, it isn't hidden away in their room but is proudly displayed downstairs along with their parents' toys. On the following page you will catch a glimpse of childish splendor—a white feathery boa, left over from the girls' New Year's Eve finery. Upstairs in Patti and Karl's room, prominently displayed on top of a family heirloom secretary, is a small fuzzy turtle, a present from Sheena. And if a picture is worth a thousand words, then the one drawn by Sami of each member of the family and taped right next to the front door certainly says a lot. To me it says this house belongs to Patti, Karl, Sheena, and Sami.

Left: Patti had always wanted a Chinese lantern, but when she saw a collection of them strung together at Manaya, an eclectic boutique in Miami Beach, she knew it was the moment to buy. When she got hers home she dangled it temporarily from the wooden chandelier over the center of the table. Karl took it one step further, wiring it so it could be lit with a flickering candlelight. Yes, it's still there . . . temporarily!

51

Above: The pair of "amazing" (Patti's adjective) metal lamps were collected from Milena's Vintage Soul trove. They are vintage Mexican pieces from the Thirties or Forties, and they are among the few that Karl hasn't gotten around to wiring—but it's only been two and a half years. The shadows they will cast on the pink wall through the floral cutouts on the shades will be spectacular, and well worth the wait. The little Noah's ark floating between them was made by Karl's father.

Left: Patti's tie-dyed slips were kind of an accident. She started off dying them solid colors and was disappointed with how they looked. "They were too perfect, like my white walls were," she explains. "One day I left one in the pot without stirring it and the color came out muted. I had messed up. But when I tried it on—I woke up!" She decided to take the imperfection a little further by tie-dying some slips. The first batch was perfection—or rather imperfection, just what Patti was looking for.

Above: Patti's "waiting room" is the room where "all the things I bring home are waiting to be fixed." In it are a couple of $2 straw baskets decorated with flower motifs, collected at thrift stores.
Left: On the grassy green wall of the waiting room, a shell sconce, an $8 yard sale find, supports a pair of Karl's garden prints. The oil above it was $4 at a Salvation Army thrift store. Patti loves all the little frogs and lizards hidden throughout her home.

When Patti started painting her walls, she had no technique in mind. If the paint started to drip, she let it. People were astounded at the mess. She liked it. Eventually, she developed a non-technique technique. She moved through each room, dripping and mixing colors. In the bedroom (see page 57), she mixed red and fuchsia. On the walls of her make-believe boutique, left, she decided to bring a little bit of the outdoors in with a grassy green. It took doses of chartreuse, yellow, and Jell-O green to come up with just the color she had been dreaming of.

Above: The romance of light and color pervades every corner of the living room. The little chandelier dripping with crystals was brass when they picked it out at Blackwatch in Forest Hills, New York, for $40.

Right: "You have to have faith" is Patti's junker mantra. The old magnolia print hanging above the futon and strung with party lights from Sheena's birthday was a find on Lincoln Road for about $25. The large mirror was from Blackwatch of Forest Hills, New York, for $30. She and Karl transformed it with a base of white paint, adding gold on the "bumps." They could easily have sold it at Fly Boutique or Vintage Soul (they sometimes refurbish their finds for resale) for $400 or more, but having hauled it so far, they decided it was a keeper. The wrought-iron planters from the Forties are covered in black roses. Patti spotted them at Vintage Soul almost the first day it opened. The child's chair with the wood plank seat was part of a set of six that she and her junking buddy, Jean Marie (the owner of Fly Boutique), had to have for $20 at Lincoln Road Collectibles. Jean Marie was having a baby, so she took one, Patti took another for Sheena and Sami, and they sold the other four. Sometimes a junking deal works out for everybody.

Leave it to Patti to fall in love with a waterlogged print of the Blessed Mother and Child! The picture had been priced at $75 before water damaged it. When Patti expressed an interest, the surprised dealer from the Salisbury Antique Center, Salisbury, Connecticut, let her have it for $10. "I don't think I would have bought it before it was distressed," she admits. "It has a tie-dyed quality to it."

Above: As you exit Patti and Karl's crimson bedroom, you duck under a hot pink Hawaiian hibiscus sarong (a $1 find) twisted over the doorway to provide privacy at times. The oversized cream French tulip was photographed by Patti years earlier when she was trying to figure out what to do with her life. The gold Florentine shelf below it was found after she discovered her skills as a junker; it cost $15 at the Lincoln Road Collectibles.
Right: Against the crimson red wall of the bedroom, a modern Italian galvanized metal lamp rests on a pair of Florentine Forties nesting tables scooped up at the Lincoln Road flea market more than five years ago for $90. "The lamp," Patti explains, "is not something we would have picked out for ourselves." It was actually an expensive prop she had found for a shoot she and Karl were collaborating on in New York in 1986. At the end of the shoot, the client gave it to them. A tiny shell remnant reminds us where we are.

Above: A palm tree view confirms we really are in Miami Beach! The little love seat under it went for $50 at a yard sale. The pair of purple crushed velvet chairs are from Vintage Soul, $110, and the pair of very high heels on the table in the foreground are Seventies icons picked up for $1.

Left: Though the inhabitants of this house love to move things around, Patti is confident that this oval painting of deep red roses will remain where it is. An oil from the Twenties, it is signed as well as English, yet despite this pedigree it cost only $10 at a yard sale.

Amid red walls and red roses, a delicate Victorian secretary lined with personal mementos stands like a little shrine to love of family in Karl and Patti's upstairs bedroom. The desk was a present from Karl's mother ten years ago. The black pocket-book installed on top of it at the far left belonged to Patti's mother. Patti uses it as a jewelry box. The pair of hand-painted wooden letter holders filled with family snapshots was a $10 find on Lincoln Road. And if all of this wasn't enough, there is the dried drippy backdrop of Patti's first painted wall, a valentine to the whole family!

Like a postcard to wear.

Along Northwest 27th Avenue you'll discover one big thrift store after another. King Pawn is hard to miss!

A plastic fan for $1 from Little Havana.

A $5 view of Miami Beach, hunted down at Stone Age Antiques. I collect a cityscape from each city I visit.

A Cuban version of a Dollar General on Calle Ocho in Little Havana. I loved the bright plastic storage bins.

An old-time collector in Miami Beach has decorated the exterior of his anchor fence with designs of plastic tape.

An arrow of red plastic tape on a junkyard gate.

Three pairs of plastic jeweled

A $1 Miami toy collection.

A typical mural decorating the wall of one of Little Havana's restaurants. I wish I could have brought it home.

A tower of junk at Stone Age.

Ballerina lamps discovered in the cavernous clutter of Douglas Garden Thrift Store, returned to center stage.

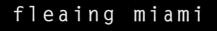

fleaing miami

Because Miami has such a transitory population, both old and young, there is a lot of stuff sold at yard

Treat yourself to good Cuban food at El Exquisito on Calle Ocho (8th Street) in Little Havana.

Two generations of the Stone Age Antiques family.

On South River Drive, you'll find a warehouse of lost treasure. Stone Age Antiques is the ultimate junk gallery.

$2 souvenir of Florida frame.

sandals. Cost: $2.50 a pair.

Neptune holds court at American Salvage.

A sidewalk fashion show on the streets of Little Havana. Not vintage, but cheap!

It may not be pretty, but Thrift City has just about anything you want: an air conditioner, perhaps?

A Fifties inner tube preserved in an old Miami Beach variety store for $1 and restored to its former glory.

Ballet booty being transported to the car.

For sale at Stone Age: acres of old nautical rope, a yellow fireplug, and unseaworthy furniture.

Salvage weathering at Stone Age.

sales and hauled off to warehouse-sized thrift shops. The main event is the Lincoln Road Mall held every Sunday.

I get a very good feeling when I walk into one of those ubiquitous office supply depots, familiar landmarks everywhere. In the age of the laptop and Palm Pilot, they are the closest thing to the old five-and-dime stores, devoted to the most basic needs of the nine-to-five life. There is something truly comforting about pushing a cart through aisles lined with high-rise shelves brimming with stacks of crisp yellow legal pads, multitudes of envelopes, boxes of No. 2 yellow pencils, paper clips in all sizes and colors, staplers, pencil sharpeners, tape dispensers, scissors, a barrage of storage trays, and organizers for everything. When I round a corner and see a mountain of classic marbleized black-and-white school notebooks, I am encouraged that the most basic and authentic tools of our daily work life will survive.

If you walk into my office in a glossy high-rise on Madison Avenue, you will find I have not totally conceded to the Microsoft world. Though I have traded in my typewriter for a laptop, I have not given up my beautiful old rolltop desk or a big fat wind-up alarm clock (like the ones seen on page 66). I exult in tracking down old but useful office staples in alternative supply markets. Recently I found a beautiful old stamp holder, a paper cutter (see page 65), and a very worldly desk lamp (page 71) at a couple of my favorite city flea markets. On a junking trip to Los Angeles, I pulled into Orange (see above, far left, and page 65), a new and stylish office supply boutique, and added a hot pink enameled Rolodex to my uncommon office supplies. Don't let work get you down: go out and splurge on 118 pencils for 10¢ each, as I did one Sunday at a flea market on 26th Street. They sit like office candy on my desk, and for any of my stalwart colleagues who still chew on pencils, they're free!

Above, left to right: Orange, a hip supplier of refurbished office supplies in Los Angeles; flea market office storage; Two Jakes in Brooklyn offers a warehouse of everything old and useful to outfit your work life; thrift shops, like Call Again in New York, offer one-stop sidewalk shopping.
Left: I can't believe I bought the whole thing! A pencil holder full—118 at last count—for half off the listed price at the 26th Street flea market.
Preceding pages: A cache of secondhand supplies sorted in the rows of a utility metal shelf. More details on page 66.

Clockwise from top left: 1. Handy scratch pads decorated with original watercolor office art by Inga Jake, wife of one of the partners of Two Jakes. This is a warehouse filled with used office furniture, not unlike those she has portrayed, in the Greenpoint section of Brooklyn, New York. **2.** A double dose of vintage Carter's ink, one for me and one for son Carter, $1 each, plus a souvenir pencil of the Empire State Building, $5, housed in the little army green metal storage unit, $2, seen on page 67 and found at the Grand Bazaar on New York's West 27th Street. **3.** Though this line-up of vintage staplers at Orange, Los Angeles, are not for sale (they're props), plenty are! (See page 68 for more details.) **4.** Cool office, you think? Think again and then head for Two Jakes in Brooklyn, New York. Started three years ago by Dave and Mike Jake—the two Jakes—its huge inventory of used office furniture and accessories was inherited from the business their father and grandfather started in the Thirties. **5.** A 50¢ one-drawer file from a yard sale. Why wouldn't you check out the alternatives first? **6.** A pair of green lampshades, $5, from a city flea market table. See one at work on the following page. **7.** I couldn't resist this old green paper cutter, $5, at the SoHo flea market. **8.** A pair of clocks created out of a propeller and fan guard. Mounted on a cinderblock wall at Two Jakes, they are part of a unique collection by Michael Whitney ranging in price from $100 to $135. **9.** A butcher-block-topped file cabinet on sale outside a used furniture store in lower Manhattan. **10.** Remember typewriters? I tested this not so old Smith-Corona at Two Jakes in Brooklyn. You can pick one up for between $50 and $125. **11.** First I bought the swivel stamp holder for about $20, then the stamps for about $2 each at the SoHo flea market. **12.** Steel City? Would that be the city where these paper clips originated, Pittsburgh, Pennsylvania? It was the unique graphics on the box, 75¢ at The Rummage Shoppe, Millerton, New York, that clinched its purchase.

3.

4.

11.

12.

100 No. 1
STEEL
CITY
GEM PAPER CLIPS
MFD. BY I. & M. SUFRIN, PGH., PA., U.S.A.

7.

6.

5.

Clockwise from right: 1. The handmade desk, quite tall, is one I think Ernest Hemingway might have chosen, since I've read he liked to write standing up. I purchased it years ago at an upstate flea market for about $20. The dangling bulb above it is protected by one of the green metal shades, seen on the preceding page at the New York City flea market, where I claimed them for $3. The gray metal drafting chair is one of several I picked up at a tag sale for about $5 apiece. **2.** Coming in for a closer look, we note a bizarre penholder crafted of three wooden blocks of varying sizes, affixed one on top of the other and anchored at each corner with a marble. It was a rare find at The Rummage Shoppe, Millerton, New York, for $2.50. The globe lamp was a $15 souvenir from a trip to the Grand Bazaar on West 25th Street in New York. The handy stand-up calendar was a customer gift from Hines Furniture & Appliance of Groesbeck, Texas, in 1954. I found it at the bottom of a box of stuff from a flea market. To the right of the penholder throne is a yellow box of State of California Standard Wire Staples, 50¢ at a garage sale in New York. The olive drab stapler by Arrow was part of an office quartet scooped up at Rentparty in Cambridge, Massachusetts, for $5. The makeshift pencil holder to the rear was actually designed for poker chips. The pencil sharpener on the edge is totally shot with rust. Guess that's why I got it for a quarter! **3.** The cool pointy glasses, Fifties style, were from a tag sale collection spotted at a San Francisco flea market for $2. **4.** A leaning tower of file cabinets, topped off by a little bell livened up with orange paint, was spotted at a sidewalk sale in Boston for $1.50. The drawers on top of the file cabinet are tagged "Elect." They were retrieved out of a junk shop in NYC for $5. The necklace of wooden rulers (18 in all!) was bought at the SoHo flea market for $10. **5.** An Ajustrite stool adjusts up and down to the proper height required by the sitter. **6.** I found Paul Goldberger's *The Skyscaper,* published in 1982, for $8.50 at a secondhand book stall—in Manhattan, of course.

THE SKYSCRAPER
PAUL GOLDBERGER

6.

5.

4.

3.

MEMO

A still life of office design centered on the ingenious stapler: this one, manufactured by the Markwell Mfg. Co. in New York, New York, was $1. Gathered around it, like swimmers in an Esther Williams water spectacular, are a collection of second-hand scissors, for $1 to $5 from various flea markets. The $3 tag sale toolbox behind them, seen in a large collection on page 32, stores two dozen small glass bottles.

Above: "Marvel" is embossed on this classic steel two-hole paper puncher. For the $1 I paid for it, that is exactly what it is—a marvel of utility sculpture!

Right: If you're not sure what this gray plastic robot look-alike thing is, check it out again, open, in the picture opposite. It's trademarked Kin-Dex, a poor cousin of the famed Rolodex, perhaps? It cost me twenty pennies at The Rummage Shoppe, Laurie Higgins's bargain basement thrift shop for office supplies in Millerton, New York.

I was there on opening day when the Walker Evans exhibit opened at New York City's Metropolitan Museum in February 2000. When I walked past those hundreds of images that I have known and loved in books only, I'll confess that there were tears in my eyes. Pausing in front of the kitchens and bedrooms of the sharecroppers celebrated in *Now Let Us Praise Famous Men*, I was struck by Evans's love of humble things. Would he have loved an old cast-iron hole puncher, like the one seen above, or a plastic Rolodex file, seen at right, or a Scotch heavy-duty tape dispenser, seen on the opposite page? I like to think so.

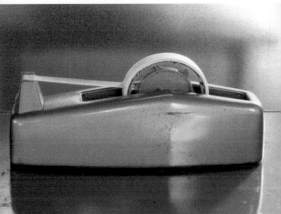

Above: A far cry from the plastic disposable tape dispensers I gobble up: the Scotch heavy-duty tape dispenser is weighted so you can quickly disengage an inch of tape without lifting another finger. It was $4 at the Call Again Thrift Shop, New York City.

Left: A Fifties gooseneck desk lamp peers down at a roundup of small office helpers poised on the top of a gray metal portable typewriter table. The desk lamp, more at home on a student's desk than an office worker's, was $1 on a tag sale table. (It doesn't work.) The Kin-Dex, seen before on the opposite page, was 20¢ at The Rummage Shoppe; the calendar from Joe's Tire Shop in Waterbury, Connecticut, was a typical giveaway in the Fifties, I paid 75¢ for it at a sidewalk tag sale. The deluxe Boston Vacuum Mount pencil sharpener is doing a job on some of those 118 pencils I bought at the 26th Street flea market, on page 62. The hole puncher at the back makes a great paperweight since it lost its punch. The old typewriter table, sort of like a sidecar on wheels, was around $10 at the Grand Bazaar on West 25th Street in New York city. My son Carter has its twin in his apartment, page 24. He uses it as a mobile bedside table.

Above: A set of four Merco glass canisters with stainless steel tops, just the way I found them at the Georgia Avenue Thrift Store Center in Washington, D.C. They were $6.96 for the set.
Right: Instead of storing doctor's supplies, these jars are now home to office items.

A junker friend of mine, Annie Groer, a writer for the *Washington Post* (see her political junk on page 74), suggested I check out the Georgia Avenue Thrift Store Center. My first spin through was a little disappointing. But then I spotted the quartet of canisters seen at right. In all my years of junking I had never come across the likes of them before. But here were those familiar jars designating their original contents: bandages, tongue depressors, cotton, and gauze. I had other plans for them, as you can see at right: thumbtacks, No. 2 yellow pencils, tape dispensers, and boxes of film.

"JFK" looks on at the White House and the Capitol. It's a rug/banner made in Italy from rag fiber, $20.

Check out the truck for hidden treasures.

The Georgetown Flea Market on U Street is fairly new. I found a cool JFK scrapbook for $10.

Junking under the sun

Yellow cabs & fleas in Washington.

Parking lots, normally empty on the week-end, are filled to capacity with truck-loads of junk.

Elephants give the party away. The guy? Ike.

Souvenir ashtrays are ubiquitous at flea markets. You can pick them up for about $10 apiece.

D.C. pennants, $3 at the original Georgetown flea on Wisconsin Avenue and S Street. Sundays, 9 to 5.

Tiny treasures offered up in pin-up baggies.

Clinton friends brought back from Moscow for $20, as a gift to a politico collector, Annie Groer.

Shopping basket booty:

fleaing the capital

Our nation's capital has much more to offer than the tour of the Washington Monument and all those other

D.C. in January.

Annie Groer's nesting presidents, made in Russia, discovered at Capital Coin for $55.

Portrait of JFK from an estate sale for $12.

Check out page 72 to see one of my favorite finds, picked up at the Georgia Avenue Thrift Center.

A street vendor in Georgetown well stocked with souvenir trinkets— a Lady of Guadalupe medal for $2.

Ike & Mamie plate is a yard sale souvenir, $8.

One of the many thrift stores in the D.C. community. This one has a parking lot— what treasure!

Washington Monument, only $6.

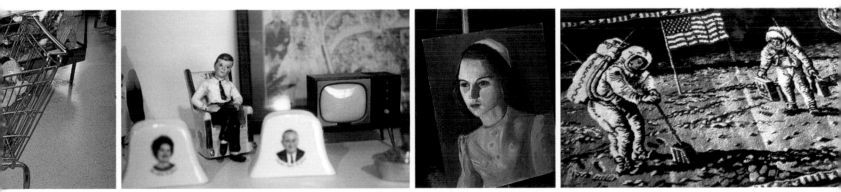

eight things for under $30!

Salt and peppers of the earth: Lady Bird, Lyndon, and JFK in a rocking chair. From Annie Groer's kitchen stock.

Jackie O? Just $4 at the original Georgetown flea.

Like JFK in the top row, this moon-landing commemorative rug/banner is a gift from Annie Groer.

historical stops. Next time, tour the flea markets and thrift shops and bring back a whole different breed of political souvenirs.

BEAT OF
A DIFFERENT
DRUMMER

Randy Saunders picked up his first pair of drumsticks when he was four. That was in Ohio. Almost twenty years later he picked up a new pair, plus a full set of drums to go with them, in a music store in the city of drummers—San Francisco. But when he recently moved into his present apartment, on the second floor of one of those classic San Francisco turreted row houses, the drums had long been in storage. "I never had space or money to rent a studio to house them in," he says. His new roommate, Jereny Blas, an aspiring photographer who had lived in the apartment for seven years, was ready for a change. When Randy moved in they decided to sell all the stuff they didn't want, gut the place, and start over. Ideally, they would both have loved a spacious, airy loft. Realistically they couldn't afford one. Instead, they created a space that feels like one. The doors between the bedroom and living room were ripped out and replaced by sheer fabric suspended from a wire grommeted along the ceiling, which gave the room industrial definition—exactly what they were looking for! Different shades of paint played a role in creating the illusion of more space. When the time came to bring in furniture and decorative objects, they chose pieces that contributed to their industrial aesthetic and, just as important, served a purpose. The large green sofa, seen on page 79, provides plenty of seating, serves as a guest bed, and offers inspiration for the paint tones of the walls. A friend of Jereny's provided the black leather shampoo chair. When they added side tables to the list of "must finds," Randy heard the distant beat of his almost forgotten drums!

Left and opposite: If you peer out of Randy and Jereny's front windows, you'll catch what looks like a mirror reflection of the 1920s apartment building they live in. (Because they're on a hill—a San Francisco bonus—it feels like they're at least a floor higher than their two stories.) Way back in the alley a gray mongrel dog mural guards the neighborhood. The shampoo chair came from a going-out-of-business hair salon for $25. Randy saw a table with legs that reminded him of drum legs. He retrieved two of his drums from storage and set the first one—a snare drum—next to the chair. The other went into the bedroom (seen on page 87). Jereny loved the idea, and added a beaker, picked up at a liquidator store for $1, filled with a gold-tinted water, to the drum in the living room. Randy's original drum set (five drums and four cymbals) cost him about $800—new. It new's not what you had in mind, particularly if your intention is decoration, not performance, then be sure to check out the Yellow Pages for secondhand musical instruments, or call the nearest music store and ask about castoffs. Classifieds or an edition of the *Penny-saver* might also turn up something.

Above and left: A long view of the living room, anchored by triple windows outlined in white. The avocado-green velvet sofa under the large number 3 was picked up at a local Goodwill store for $65. Not only does it provide plenty of comfortable seating, as well as a guest bed for unexpected guests, but it was the inspiration for the various shades of green wall paint. The coffee table was a restored piece from Swallow Tail on Polk Street. It is actually the most expensive piece in the apartment ($50 more than the bamboo tree). Sharing a disciplined view of decorating, Randy and Jereny elected to put very little on the walls. Their style comes from the mix of old and new, with a reverence for both. The large black 3 hovering above the end of the green sofa and to the right of the bamboo tree (the most expensive purchase in their apartment—$300) is an exception to their less-is-more aesthetic. A numerologist friend interpreted "3" as "creativity." "That's why we have three stools lined up under the windows," confesses Randy. The window to the left of the 3 is purposely bare. When they decided against drapes, the shade was substituted, but not just for privacy. On special occasions, or just for a little creative fun, a vintage slide projector seen on top of an army-green locker (page 81) is in position to project an image onto the shade, now a screen. During holiday festivities they project Christmas scenes; at birthday celebrations, they use funny childhood pictures from the birthday victim's past. Though it was the avocado-green sofa that inspired the shades of green on the 12-foot-high walls of their living room, color coordination was only one consideration. Another was to use color as a space enhancer. Instead of choosing just one color of green, they chose three. The lighter, pale yellow green, as seen at left, was applied to the bigger walls; the two darker shades, like the brownish green seen on the following pages, was applied to the smaller walls. The result: a 14½ by 12½-foot room that appears much roomier and very creative.

Above: Anything that relates to photography, such as the manual slide projector displayed on a cinder block pedestal, speaks to Jereny's love of the photographic image. This one, manufactured by Vivid in the Fifties, was $15 at Urban Ore in Berkeley, and "It works!" declares Jereny.

Right: The cinder block pedestal—inspired, says Randy, by Donald Judd—was the end product of a cinder block sale initiated by a neighbor's move. Being neighborly, they bought a bunch of blocks for 50¢ apiece. A single block, seen on the opposite page on the floor to the left of the locker, holds a glass vase. Since then, the vase has become the home of goldfish. The schoolhouse clock positioned above the projector is a vintage-inspired new version from Pottery Barn.

Above: After they turned their 12-foot-long coat closet into an office (see page 84), Randy and Jereny were faced with the dilemma of most city dwellers—not enough storage space. They met the challenge with great aplomb (and courageous thrift), by heading off to Urban Ore, a favorite salvage stop & shop. Within minutes they had spotted a tall, thin pair of metal school lockers. The price was right—$75—as was the color—regulation army green! And along with storage space for jackets and bags, they got the bonus display space topside. First up, on the far left, another Urban Ore find—a photographic timer for $10. The $15 vintage Westinghouse fan, from the St. Francis thrift shop on Pine Street, is rarely put into service, since living up on a hill provides all the air-conditioning they need. The low black Kodak carousel projector, seen at far right, was $100, from a pawn shop on Sutter Street. It provides the perfect projection of images to the window shade seen on page 78. On the floor, to the left of the closed locker, is the single cinder block pedestal holding the glass vase which is now home to three goldfish. Seen to the right of the far locker is the entrance to the bedroom, seen in full on page 77. The sheer white curtain pulls across a taut wire secured within the doorway to address privacy issues when the green sofa offers guest accommodation.

"I think they're school stools, the kind used in chemistry classes," says Randy, of the trio lined up under the three windows in the living room. Of the five purchased (from Urban Ore, again) for $5 apiece, only one swivels. The seltzer bottle has to date found no permanent location. Today it perches on the middle stool, looking a bit like a glass penguin. It was bought from a vintage collection sold at Pottery Barn for $69.

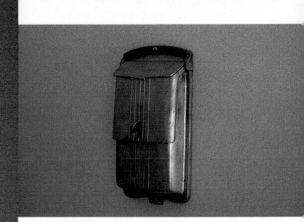

Opposite, clockwise from left: What was once a walk-in coat closet is now a highly efficient work space. And that door has been given new distinction as well, with a double dose of cool accessories from X21, a modern supply shop in the Mission District of San Francisco. On top is a stainless steel instructor sign, $16, and below, affixed like a modern knocker, is an old film reel, $10. Pulled up to the glass countertop supported by two stacks of cinder blocks is another of the $5 school stools seen on the previous pages. The clip-on lamps directing light to the ceiling cost $8 at Brownies, a hardware store around the corner, and the hanging shelves are from Target. Canvas curtains partition off more storage to the right and left of the counter. The magazine rack outside the door is actually a towel ladder. The box of reels, not unlike the one on the office door, was offered for sale at the SoHo flea market, 3,000 miles away, for around what Randy and Jereny paid—$10.

Above: "You've got mail," not e-mail but real mail, in the little stripped-down, spray-painted mailbox attached to the inside of the closet office door. Found at a local shop for $10, it holds unpaid bills.

Left: The pipes attached to the bedroom wall were originally placed to support a glass shelf to hold the carousel projector. When the logistics for that failed, the pipes remained as slightly out-of-place sculptures, until the day Jereny brought home the old Canon movie projector he picked up at a Goodwill shop for $25. It fit perfectly and matched the mood and era of the black-and-white radiator below.

Above: Over the bed, spelling out the letters of America's classic soft drink, is a rusty sign dragged home from Another Time, a salvage store in Oakland, for $50.
Opposite: The beat continues in the bedroom with a drum converted into a bedside table. With great style and function, the three-legged Floor Tom adjusts to whatever height is needed. The nylon drumhead can be tightened if it sags by turning the screws around the perimeter with a little drum key. The drumhead can also be replaced (decorators, take note!) by a clear one or by one of just about any color. The clock and candle are new; the Asian water plant is of much more venerable lineage.

I have always been cautious about hanging things over my bed. If I lived in San Francisco, I might be even more careful, given its penchant for middle-of-the-night tremors. Choose something that is not too heavy, and avoid glass at all costs. Never trust the hanging wire attached to old paintings; chances are it's as old as the art! Usually, however, it's not the wire that's untrustworthy, but the eye screws and the old wood they're screwed into. Rehang with a multi-strand, 24-gauge wire. If the wood of the frame seems too soft, tack some wooden strips on top of it, or consider replacing the frame, particularly if it is big and heavy. To hang a piece as long as the Coca-Cola sign, consider using two nails or hanging hooks, spread apart to share the weight. Always check the solidity of the wall surface you're counting on. Picture hangers are most reliable. Wallboard requires a toggle or wing bolt for maximum security. When in doubt, hang your art on the wall where you can wake up in the morning and really enjoy it!

Signs of the '60s, a vintage Volkswagen bus, decals and all, parked in the lot of the Alemany Flea Market.

Inside a chain link fence — Heaven! It's a junker's no-frills picnic, spread out neatly on the parking lot concrete.

A rough linen money bag; three for $5.

A quartet of frosted souvenir

Flights of fancy, 50¢.

Recording my finds. At the end of the day I store the snapshots, prices, and details in my junker's scrapbook.

Searching for souvenirs of California, I came across a license plate, but passed it up for the set of glasses, above.

Flea market Fashion Rules!

Vintage hubcaps from the '40s and '50s look like metal Frisbees. Bought one for my son Carter for $5.

Be sure to play the Dealer's game — Haggle!

Ordinary drawer fill looks so tantalizing before coffee!

Rows of treasure compose a weird art exhibit.

I coveted this bug-formance

fleaing san francisco

San Francisco is the junker's paradise! But I had so much fun at the Alemany Flea Market,

highballers cost me $18.

A "Bedazzled," bejeweled gun for 50¢.

A *Star Trek* mannequin's head, $10.

Time for a tune-up? A collection of colorful oil cans — yours for the taking at the Alemany "garage" sale!

Big City transport

Flower Power Decals!

My rain or shine, waterproof messenger bag.

In California you can count on a great car show right in the flea market parking lot. Load her up!

My fantasy word processor, $12.

Parking meter lamp base, $45

license plate big-time.

An old army trunk stamped with its own address. Another kind of Big City souvenir for $18.

Dapper Dealer at Work?

The Alemany Flea Market is open on Sundays. Setup is at six A.M. It's a quick ride after breakfast at Mama's.

held every Sunday in a large lot about 15 minutes from San Francisco, that I devoted all the space to my own private tour. The rest of my junking spots (and there are many!) you'll find in the Junk Guide, page 234.

89

STILL LIFE

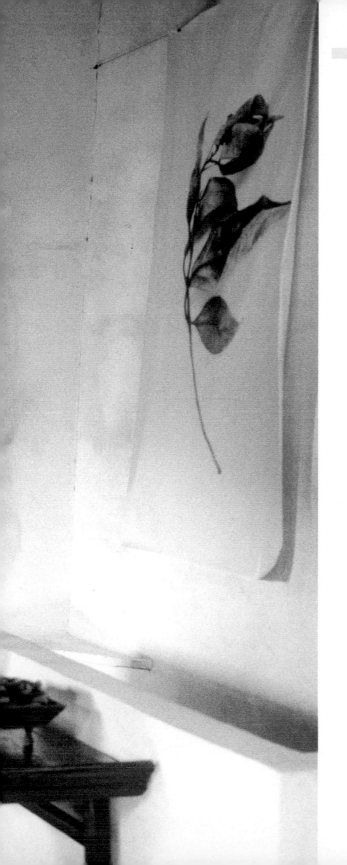

The ad read "Old World charm," and that was what the 200-year-old building, camouflaged in thick blooming vines and located on the Lower West Side of New York City, promised Don Freeman. He rented two floors—one to use as his photography studio and the other as his home. That was six years ago, and under his sensitive eye the charm has grown totally into his own. "I never wanted the place to have a look," he states resolutely. By that he means a French, or Southwestern, or shabby English look. He never went out purposely to find something like a lamp, for example, but would instead go and take a walk and find ten old frames left on the street. During a two-year stint in Paris, he fell in love with the French flea markets and the luxury of buying big things like a bed. After resettling in New York, he continued to travel back to Paris for work, but no more beds. He had to be content with bringing back small souvenirs—a dish, a cup, a book. This discipline partially explains why after all this time his home is still spare, dominated by roughly plastered walls and uneven, unwaxed wooden floors. Some of his collected objects resemble the still lifes he shoots professionally. A stack of three of his favorite books (see page 98), on the photographer Alfred Stieglitz, Russian icon painters, and the architect Luis Barrigan, speak to some of his inspiration.

Opposite: Halfway up the narrow wooden staircase you are greeted by the faint shadow of twelve-year-old Arp, Don's French bulldog. Colette, one of his favorite writers, had six!
Left: The funny baroque plaster mirror created by a friend of Don's less than a year ago, the spartan Japanese table found in a shop in the East Village, and one of his own photographic images hanging above the stairway preach a strong message of global eclecticism.
Preceding pages: The grappa bottles, seen at the far left, were props in a still life for an English interiors magazine. They were appropriated by Don and installed in his own personal still life. See page 102 for more details.

Don gave up his studio floor when he discovered that living and working in the same building was a little confining. He then moved his flat file cabinet into his living space. Though it is a functional piece, for storing his photographs and tearsheets, it provides a generous surface to display three disparate but loved treasures—a little cream bowl, a flea market lamp, and one of his own blueprint photographs of a statue at the Vatican Museum. Puddling beside it is 14 feet of natural linen painter's canvas, attached to a track on the ceiling above. Nightly it is pulled across the room to create a sleeping nook for Don and Arp. The unframed bed, seen to the right of it, is folded up in the morning and hidden in a closet to extend the space and hospitality to visiting friends. Two silver leather poufs and a Chinese chest offer an improvised chat room against a framed back-drop of Don's mysterious peonies photographed in 1989.

Right: The flat files—he has never found a better set—were custom-made at David Davis, an art supply center in the East Village, for $250. The unsigned lamp, credited as one of his best finds ever at the 26th Street flea market, has still not been identified eight years later. The light of his life cost him $350. The delicate wire lantern balanced on the ledge is the twin to the one seen on the preceding page. They were gifts from the owners of Shi in SoHo.

Above: One of three skylights, trapdoors to the sky, that were reopened when Don took residence.
Left: The pair of Turkish poufs upholstered in silver leather and stuffed with Polartec scraps were found at Dosa on Thompson Street. The lacquered woven Chinese chest was a find at Thirty Bond in the Village for $100. You can find delicate designs by Ted Muhling, like the candlestick holder he gave to Don, in his SoHo design studio on Greene Street.
Below: Let sleeping dogs (like Arp!) lie in a patch of sun from the skylight above.

95

Above: A drafting stool was retrieved from an early morning forage at the 26th Street flea market.

Right: A mantelpiece salvaged from the street not far from Don's front door supports three empty clay pots found much farther away in a Paris flea market. They complement Don's image of night magnolias, framed beside them. The Belgian linen curtain, to the left, is placed strategically to alter the space. Don simply throws it into the washing machine. Wrinkles are an important feature!

It isn't surprising that a photographer who prints his images on blueprint paper, and is happiest when they have aged to a parchment yellow, would want to live in a muted landscape filled with organic textures and subtle hues. Case in point: the palette at right, with a stone-colored Belgian linen curtain, a mantelpiece fragment the color of butter-cream candy, terra-cotta pots washed with organic residues, a pale bone-colored frame surrounding the blueprint magnolias, and the earthy texture of hand-plastered walls.

Opposite: Another found mantel fragment rests on the floor because it's too heavy to hang. It subs as low-slung seating and a sunny spot for lanky topiaries and prized books. The wood pedestal, a far cry from the stack of firewood piled next to the fireplace, was a gift from the artist Christian Liagre.

Left: The mirror over the fireplace, reflecting Don's branches, seen above the stairway on page 93, was created from layers of silver-leafed glass by Maureen Fullam. The Eames rocker before it, a favorite winter spot, was "not cheap," Don admits, "but the perfect color." Though there are less expensive versions to be had, he insisted on this Fifties version imbued with a patina of age, like everything else in his home.

the unshining:
floors that have
endured the test of time
and no varnish

Don's 200-year-old floors have never seen a touch of varnish, just lots of soapy washings. The only shine in his very matte apartment are his two mirrors and the aluminum chairs hanging off the wall in the food preparation area (see page 101). To preserve the dull beauty of his wall-to-wall floorboards, he is committed to a regimen of energetic sweeping and vacuuming, particularly over the wider cracks, and weekly moppings with soap and water. Stains are an inevitable curse. The one seen on the opposite page, near the woodpile, is the landmark of a great pot roast that never made it to the table. Arp will testify to its splendor!

Above: A view out the back of Don's apartment reveals neighboring balconies and a garden decorated with an urban artifact—an old Texaco sign.

Right: The trio of chairs floating above the windows were found at least ten years ago. The black metal Knoll chair he picked up at the 26th Street flea market for $100. The pair of aluminum Fifties classics were offered at a sale during the renovation of Carnegie Hall for $25 each. The bouquetlike chandelier was caught at Thirty Bond, for $75.

Is this the dwelling of a modern Shaker? Or the home of a man with an appreciation of the practical and meticulous Shaker sensibility? The chairs, seen at right, went up on the walls when floor space was tight. The ladder leaning against the pebble-colored plaster in the back of the apartment was there upon Don's arrival. He respects its usefulness, its age, and the design contrast it provides in the lineup of modern chairs. The romantic postscript to all of this is the creamy candlelit chandelier dangling from the ceiling in the midst of unfinished wood, rough plaster, and an urban view from the curtainless windows.

Above: A view from the bathroom, seen on the following pages, to the sink niche, seen close-up at right.
Right: Shoehorned into a back corner of the apartment, just beyond the wall of chairs and ladders seen on the preceding pages, is Don's large sink, purchased at a kitchen supply warehouse in the Bowery for $150.

The shelves seen at right—unlike their counterparts built in nearby to store tableware, cutlery, pots and pans, and all the tools of cooking—pay no homage to the kitchen. They lodge souvenirs from random photo shoots, scavenger hunts at flea markets in London, Paris, and New England, and journeys to far-flung places like Joshua Tree National Monument in California. Represented are favorites that could have multiplied into entire collections of chess sets, birdcages, glass bottles, desert rocks, wooden boxes, picture frames, books, and etching plates. Instead, Don chose restraint, and collects a special one of everything that he likes.

102

Above: The white enamel medical cabinet storing bathroom stuff was rescued from The Lively Set, a store in the West Village beset by a celebrity buyer set on owning every vintage medical cabinet. (Can you guess who?) Her collector's lust unfortunately drove the price up to $1,000! You may get lucky with these now-popular items at an out-of-town flea market or auction, but don't count on it.

Left: In the center of this little bathroom shrine is a glass vase from a Paris flea market stuffed with a newspaper photograph by one of Don's favorites, Bill Brandt. Casting a triple reflection is an old fold-up travel mirror, an easy bring-home from a Paris flea for $12. A 25¢ flea market replica of the Eiffel Tower stands proudly in New York. (When he lived in Paris, Don displayed a replica of the Empire State Building.) The miniature French hat stand is related to the one seen earlier on the shelf above the sink. Don's framed color print of wax fruit, shot for a German magazine, is a bulletin board for a postcard portrait of Arp, and a Russian icon painting from the 15th century. The little sculpted hand to the right of the mirror, and the one attached to the chain hanging on the hat stand at left, are both by the artist Gabriella Kiss.

Right: Until recently the Adam Hats Factory, located in Dallas's historic jazz district— Deep Ellum—was just another derelict remnant of better times and better hat days. In the early 1900s, it was the home of a Ford motor plant, and a couple of decades later, until men's hats went out of style (thank you, JFK), it had been a thousand-hats-a-day factory. Today its six floors of industrial space have been converted into lofts for a disparate group of creative home owners, One of them, Mark Clay, an interior designer and sophisticated junker (sort of!), lives on the ground floor with lots of light concrete floors, exposed brick walls, and just the right stuff. Take a peek at his gymnasium-scaled space, opposite, and prepare to learn how to give your collections and your living space some quality breathing room . . . and still have fun!

INDUSTRIAL STRENGTH

Mark Clay's hat factory home is an industrial junker's paradise stripped down to concrete, brick, and a wall of windows.

Mark Clay has come a long way from the rural route in southeast Missouri where he was raised surrounded by fields of cotton. The Adam Hats Factory in the Deep Ellum section of Big D suits him just fine. In the early 1900s it was a Ford plant (you can still see the parts chute in the center of the lobby, on the next page), and then, a couple of decades later, it switched its gears to hats. By the time John F. Kennedy rode hatless down Pennsylvania Avenue to his inauguration, the factory had closed down. Mark spotted it in the '80s, all boarded up, and thought it would make the "coolest" living space. He wasn't looking for living space that time around, but when he returned to Dallas in 1997, after a stint in New York City, he saw the boards were off and a sign that read, "Now Leasing." He sacrificed a view for a parking space right outside his ground-floor door. His stock in trade (interior design) requires a lot of moving in and out. And though his office is really his car (nine times out of ten, that's where you'll reach him!) the 1,600 square feet of open space—concrete and 14-foot-high windows—is a reliable backup. He lives there, too, of course, with fewer possessions than you'd think. He assuages his collecting passion by scouring flea markets and shops for others (paying clients), nine to five. What a lucky guy!

It took climbing up a ladder in a gymnasium to retrieve the source for this large-scale fan. Mark got it from The Stadium Company in Minneapolis for $550.

Right: Like a red-and-yellow megasculpture spiraling down from the center of the new Adam Hats Factory atrium-like lobby, the original parts shaft is from the building's car-manufacturing days. According to Mark, each tenant is required to sign a waiver, along with their lease, committing to no shaft shenanigans. To date, no midnight rides have been reported.
Opposite: A boiler room door displayed like a piece of functional art on the purple wall opposite the lobby's car-parts shaft serves as yet another reminder of the building's industrial roots.

salvage salvation:
big city treasure digs

Big Cities from coast to coast are engaged in the rapid conversion of mothballed industrial sites into home and shop dwellings. (See the loading ramp entrance to Interieur Perdu in San Francisco, on page 234.) Those that do it right are saving a little piece of the past and incorporating it into the future. Sound familiar? On a smaller scale, we junkers do that every day! Carter Berg's traffic signs (see page 20), the broken water main claimed by John Bennet from a construction hole and transformed into a pedestal for his sculpture (see page 157), the hubcap art in Bobby Furst's Los Angeles backyard, all speak to the joys of urban junking. "Urban fossils" are what two creative artist/junkers call the New York City manhole covers they are turning into urban artifacts (see page 159).

If someone (a junker in particular) walked into Mark Clay's 1,600 square feet of clean space he or she might ask, "Where's the junk?" I asked that on my first visit and then quickly began to adjust my personal junker's vision to appreciate his. Junk style tends to be associated with wall-to-wall stuff, not unlike the crammed and jumbled quarters, tables, or fields from which it is retrieved. But whether they collect a lot or a little, there is something that Big City living instills in most urban foragers—a little bit or a lot of self-control. Witness Mark's "lot of" self-control throughout this section.

Left: Mimicking the metal-and-wire stairway it hangs under, an old wire grocery shelf brought back from Nashville's "Heart of the Country" antique show for $125 stores nonperishable goods. The vintage drafting chair under it, spiffed up by Legacy Trading, Dallas, cost $85. A lesson in stylish storing—floor plans rolled up in a polished milk bucket from Coco & Company, Chicago, for $75. Or substitute an old galvanized bucket from your next tag sale outing.

Opposite: To file away socks, underwear, T-shirts, workout clothes, belts, more floor plans, and "other" (see industrial ID tags opposite), Mark went for the real thing—an automotive supply company's stackable file drawer system. Designed for storing car parts (was Mark thinking of the heritage of his factory home?), the drawers are sold individually for $45 each from the Randoph Company, Chicago. They come in red, white, or green, but Mark ordered them stripped down to the metal. If you're willing to endure a few dents, check out the old office file I found for $25 at a city flea market (see page 67). Line up a series of them and you're in the storage business for a lot less.

109

Above: A view from the sleeping loft reveals Mark's secret storage weapon—a floor-to-ceiling glass shelf system supported by steel T-bars (from an iron supply yard) and white oak planks drilled into the 25-foot brick wall.

Left: Mark makes a case for keeping things out in the open—favorite books and magazines stacked and bookended with more stacks, topped by favorite things. A giant metal jack, a straw hat, a glass vase of roses, highlight rows of collected photographs, some picked up—like the anatomy study perched on the little wooden stand on the lower shelf, far right—at the Paris flea market. Tucked here and there are an assortment of files and boxes to keep smaller, less manageable things at bay. The leather box at the top left, next to the straw hat, was made by his bootmaker in Comanche, Texas. For another interpretation of shelf life, turn to page 132 and take a gander at an alternative shelf-storage solution (one of mine) set up in a ministorage unit. Or visit Anita Calero (page 199), in her ultraspare loft in New York City, where she keeps all her collections behind closed doors. There's always a solution—which is why I never ask: "Do I have a place for this?" Always, always, in my/your heart.

Making something out of nothing is an extraordinary trait, particularly if the activity becomes a stress reducer to boot. Mark's two-hour production of a giant ball of string was such a feat. "Have you ever had so much to do you could do nothing?" (I think we could all answer, "Yes!" to that.) "My state exactly when I created that giant string ball," confesses Mark. The string, actually chair caning material, was left over from a recent project. Displayed like an organic string-dispensing globe on a carved wooden pedestal created out of fallen trees by Mark's cousin (not Christian Liagre!), it stands guard at the foot of Mark's stairway to his loft haven.

Above: A utility tower of metro shelving stores entertainment options. Electrical conduits like those seen running up the brick wall at right were found in the basement and recycled into curtain rods for the long windows in the space.
Right: Most people keep their ball of twine in a kitchen drawer. Mark Clay's wouldn't fit, so he keeps it ever handy perched on a sculptural pedestal.

Left: One of the first things you notice when you enter Mark's tall, skinny loft space is the tall, skinny column of orchids blooming off the wall. They're his Hanging Gardens of Babylon, blooming out of a string of plastic IV bags. He confesses he imported the idea from a store in London, but picked his up from a local medical supply company for about $30. Attached like a liquid ladder to his exposed brick wall, they drip water to their patients at any rate Dr. Mark prescribes. He can leave home without guilt or worry. The nurse is on duty twenty-four hours a day.

Below: At last some telltale signs of Texas—a couple of pairs of cowboy boots lined up on the floor of Mark's up-top sleeping quarters. He has at least sixteen pairs, most of themcustom-made by Eddie Kimmel in Comanche, Texas. When he's not wearing them, they add a little yippee-yahoo color to the mix of black, saddle tan, camel, natural fibers, brick, and brushed metal. In the lineup, to the left of them, is what was in Mark's words "a real yucky paint-chipped chair with a ripped vinyl seat." (See, you probably thought Mark wouldn't touch such a thing—wrong!) He not only touched it, he transformed it by having the "yuck" sandblasted off to bare metal and trading the ripped vinyl for saddle leather. He found the orphan at the flea market in Canton, Texas, the first Monday of the month, for five buckaroos.

Souvenirs of the Lone Star State: Texas pennants, an illustrated saucer and postcard, and red bandanna.

Cowboy boots and a Fifties lamp at Cool Junk.

On Industrial Boulevard there's a great roundup of warehouses peddling every-thing from garden junk to salvage.

Cool Junk lives up to its name!

Stop for a junk burger!

Bettyann & Jimbo's Junkadoodle stands by their slogan, "Not just the same old same old!"

A stripped-down drafting chair at Legacy Trading.

Liberty & Sons Antiques, another big warehouse of stuff in the downtown industrial antiques center.

I snapped this handpainted mural on the side of a building at a red light on my Dallas junking roundup.

A legacy of urban cool at Legacy Trading.

Dallas lives up to its "Big D" reputation with one "big" junker's warehouse after another.

Mark Clay's most uncommon,

fleaing dallas

Though there's lots of great home-on-the-range stuff in Dallas, you can rope in just about anything there!

A wire bas-
ket, $3, to
tote junk.

The backyard at Bettyann and Jimbo's,
where you can shop in an Airstream.

Leather books to
propellers, at The
Uncommon Market.

A Texas flag painted on a piece
of corrugated metal, $24, at
Bettyann and Jimbo's.

A weathered red leather wallet of
the Lone Star State from my Dallas
junking friend, Kay Chefchis.

You'll find funk and sophisticated
junk at Legacy Trading Co. A mix of old
and new.

The purple
storefront of
Cool Junk.

A larger-
than-life
doorman.

reliable
resource
(page 230).

Housed in an old gas station, the
White Elephant Architectural & Garden
Station now pumps great garden junk!

Cool Junk: rope
a steer or just
about anything.

Deep in the heart of Texas — modern
architecture and uncommon junk.

Check out Cool Junk in sprawling Deep Ellum, warehouses of stuff in City Center, and
air-conditioned antiques malls (no sweltering outdoor flea markets) all over the city.

Ingredients: Old broom from some alley, wood from a dumpster by my laundromat (sp?), beads from Ramona Otto, glitter from the drugstore downstairs from Stephie Kasten's apartment in NYC, Stephie's old suede vest, my old but clean organic cotton socks, velvet from that time I used to make miniskirts and sell them, Scrabble sentence game from some thrift store, tin foil from leftovers, yarn from phyllis Eagle Kolaweros, I think.

love from Shari   1/00

"Man with His Lady," a piece of lost & found art by Shari, is subtitled in her handwriting "Or: life is a big dance." On the back of each of her pieces she writes out the ingredients. It's like a junker's love letter.

Is Shari Elf real? She seems to be a golden-haired fairy princess living in a lost-and-found world. To get to her palace of make-believe you must follow a narrow-hedged walkway in Venice (how perfect!), California (oh, were you hoping Italy?), until you come to a weathered white picket fence. Shari usually enters from the alley where she parks her car and does a lot of her rescue work. (See more about that on page 128.) She pushes open the door to her backyard, made of silk screen frames she gathered at her favorite recycling yard, and greets a life-size image of herself called "Shari of the Wild West." (See the preceding pages.) Shari rescues stuff out of junk shops and alleys, and as you have heard, even out of recycling yards. Her tale began in Maui, Hawaii, where she was born, and she grew up to design a line of clothes called Elfware. When she moved to Los Angeles, she was tired of making things that had to fit, so she started painting. But even princesses or Elfs have to earn a living, so she nannied, sewed for a dry cleaner, and had her own sewing business. One day two of her clients yelled at her, and she realized that she was getting yelled at for doing something she hated. That was her epiphany. She gave up the sewing and devoted herself full-time to painting and to selling "Shari's Cool Stuff" at various Los Angeles flea markets.

Opposite, clockwise from top left: Shari at the "fishies" door into her kitchen. The first one she made was inspired by a fish-shaped board she found in an alley. Another door, this one to Shari's backyard studio. She used to take the signs to the flea markets. The Elf Queen is another Shari image created out of rescued discards.
Preceding pages: Shari's back gate was framed out of a half dozen framed silk screens. The life-size Shari, at left, is called "Shari of the Wild West." Her skirt is a Formica counter, her hair is a rope belt, her hat a rusty can. The Toodles sign was a gift from her friend Ramona Otto.

Above: The living, sleeping, dining room flooded with sun. Watchful, on the bed, is a central character in Shari's world, a crocheted alligator named Bunny. She was found by Ramona in a desert thrift store for $3.50. The other alligator, to her right, is a suitor, but Bunny, according to Shari, "prefers policemen!"

Right: Shari's Fifties desk tucked into the office corner, just in from the kitchen door, cost $7 at Desert Industries, a thrift store on the way to the desert in Calimesa. The chair was found in an alley somewhere. Her most important tool is her blue princess telephone, found in a store on Abbot-Kinney Boulevard in Los Angeles for $5. She didn't know if it worked when she bought the phone. It did, and to have it in her life is "pure joy." She loves its ring and the way it dials, and, of course, the way it looks.

Even though Shari spends a lot of time working in her backyard studio, her office nook is crucial to other kinds of business, like talking to clients, paying bills in the light of her Popsicle lamp—a piece of Prison Art, she thinks—or checking out what's inside her cool "flower power" pocketbook.

A portrait of the artist as a brunette. It is one of Shari's earliest self-portraits and is framed with old boards she found in an alley in Santa Monica. (More on alley-ing on page 128). Her dress was made from a velvet castoff found at a flea market; the greenish rhinestones came off of an old fabric sample. Her pearls were from a beat-up pair found in a recycling yard (see page 129), and her hair (in need of conditioning) is made up of old broom straws. The strange sparkly dots reflected on it are from a mirrored disco ball rotating in the window, seen on the opposite page, which she got from Claire's Thrift Store on Pico Boulevard in Venice for 50¢. (To see Shari's portrait of yours truly as the Queen of Junk, see page 9.)

Left: Shari's self-portrait, assembled from bits of velvet, sequins, and broom straws. The straw letter holder filled to the brim below it was a 75¢ purchase at the Bargain Bazaar Thrift Store in Santa Monica.

Above: On the corner of Tenth and Pico in Venice, Shari is armed and ready for some thrifting at Claire's with her flower-powered pocketbook in hand. The "M" sweater she borrowed from her friend Marion quite a while ago. When anyone asks her what the "M" stands for, she answers, "Me!"

Left: Shari's black-and-white flower purse was made from an old purse she picked out at Bargain Bazaar Thrift Store on 15th Street in Santa Monica. It cost $2, and the white flowers were painted on with acrylics.

Shari got tired of sewing things that had to fit, so she started making things that fit the wonderful, crazy ideas in her head. One was buying old purses and painting designs on them. She painted a queen on the side of one of the first bags she bought; whenever she carried it outside, people would ask where she got it. Inspired by the interest, Shari started making these bags and selling them to specialty shops for $75 to $150. But this was not the art she wanted to focus on, so eventually she stopped her little bag business, and now she decorates them for herself.

123

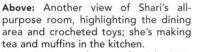

Above: Another view of Shari's all-purpose room, highlighting the dining area and crocheted toys; she's making tea and muffins in the kitchen.

Right: A star was born at the John Muir flea market in Santa Monica, and Shari found it, for $10. She thinks it was probably a Christmas yard ornament constructed out of fiberboard, covered in glitter, and shellacked. She haggled over the nice green wrought-iron garden table and four chairs with the owner of a junk truck parked on Venice and Lincoln boulevards, and eventually got the whole set for $75. The velvet thrift store pillow on the chair (she's still looking for another three) was 50¢. The little clown sack on the chair is filled with supermarket plastic shopping bags. It's cute and functional, as is the red-flowered cat on the table. This is actually a storage pouch that Shari found at a yard sale in Mara Vista for a dollar or two. The little homemade fish (out of the reach of the cat!) was a yard-sale catch for a dime. The two paintings to the right of the star are signed by Malcolm X! "I love to say to people, when they notice the artist's name, that it was a little known fact that Malcolm X was also a painter!"

Maybe it started with Bunny, the crocheted alligator, seen on her bed on page 120, but Shari Elf has a thing for crocheted toys. In her new temporary home in Kansas City, she has opened a Crochet Museum with eight shelves of handmade toys, mostly crocheted, set up in a corner of her living room. The cat and fish on the opposite page are there. The chubby clown plumped up with shopping bags is there too. Three shelves of crocheted poodles, once installed on a shelf of their own in her bathroom, are there also, as is the potholder cat seen attached to the table, to the left. Shari Elf's Crochet Museum is open only by appointment, and those are rare.

Left: The little table made out of a chunk of wood was free at a recycling center. It's just big enough to hold a party of three, including two silly angels made from upside-down Styrofoam cups found at a thrift shop nearby. One she has attached to a child's lamp over a block decoration, the other attends to the very tall bride, another thrift shop adoptee. What she loved about the lamp was the little dent in the lampshade camouflaged by a child's drawing of a face. Shari added the green fringe. The crocheted and whiskered potholder kitty attached to the front of the table guards two oversized crocheted hats. The purr-fectly beautiful cat was a present from Shari's generous friend Ramona.

Right: Through Shari's looking glass, a $10 must-have from the Santa Monica Airport flea market, we see up on the shelf to the left a prized photo of her grandmother Selma and her bowling team in Maui. The dresser it leans on came from a thrift excursion in Yucca Valley. Investment: $50. The dazzling mirrored jewelry box on the right is a piece of folk art (a yard sale birthday gift from her friend Ramona). The crocheted brown-and-white teacup was found in a Glendale thrift shop for $2. The porcelain lady with the pincushion skirt was $1.50 from the Rose Bowl flea market. Two little thrift shop boxes, in green tin and sequins and velvet, store her thrift shop jewels. The tiny Shari portrait on the wall at the left was painted on a piece of rusty metal. It sat on her dashboard on her last trip across country.

Opposite, clockwise from left: 1. What the mirror saw was a portrait of "Angel watching over us," by Shari, of course. The blue wood canvas was found in an alley; the frame was an old window frame; her wings were from a roasting pan contributed by her friend Tom; the rock dress was pieced together from landscape rocks; and the quartet of tin cans burn candles from time to time. The other portait of a little angel is a photograph of Shari as a small child, on the bedside dresser to the right of her bed. The blue lamp started off mundane and cracked. Shari took care of that by adding a funny painted-on face and a lampshade decorated with silk flower leaves. She now calls it the Life of the Party Lamp. The chest of drawers, from a recycling yard, has one broken leg in back, so she just leaned it up against the wall. **2.** On the porch at her front door stands the Welcome Lady, with arms made out of curved pieces of wood. Her flowered dress was made from a gate, and the centers of the flowers are pink milk-bottle caps. The fish swimming above her says, "Welcome!" **3.** Just inside Shari's sea-blue door, replete with a rickrack fish, are five portaits of Shari framed in the openings of a wooden-laddered ramp. **4.** After a stroll through the little hedged walkway, you know you've reached Shari's when you see what may be the only weathered picket fence in Los Angeles. The fence has been there for quite a while, but probably not as long as the house, which was built in the Twenties.

Angel watching over us

1.

2.

3.

4.

What finds await us as we turn into an unexplored alley? Those big closed trash bins offer limited access, Shari complains.

Shari discovers a child's drawing easel. She will turn the blackboard into a canvas for a portrait.

A gallery of abandoned goods lined up in a recycling yard. Large usable items are usually towed to a special spot. Bikes,

Every Big City visit has offered me new junking philosophies and methodologies. But of the nine cities I visited and all the passionate junkers I met, none can quite compare with Shari Elf and the junking journey she took me on with my good friend and diehard junker Laurie Warner Garrick and her daughter Samantha, aka "Spicey." (Their junk starred big in *Kitchen Junk* and *American Junk*, and they introduced me to their friend Shari.) Shari never drives her car down streets; instead, she takes to the alleys. Common sense would suggest that this is a good way to avoid the traffic, but common sense is not what Shari Elf has on her mind — it's a treasure hunt.

A gooseneck lamp, not unlike the one featured on page 71, for free in the recycling yard. To the right, the alley offers a pair of plastic pretties.

chairs, and TV sets are the specials of this visit. Obtaining permission is a must!

Shari finds some leftover paint in good colors. She will find a use for the paint cans as well.

In the utility corner of the recycling yard are stored brooms, rakes, and a sturdy wheelbarrow.

Above, even the smallest treasures can be discovered at the recycling yard. Shari took the blue bowling ball at left. I wanted the doghouse, seen above right. Below, Shari's treasures stacked up at the end of the day in her alley, ready for creative renewal.

STORAGE
HOUSE RULES

I have lived in New York City since I graduated from college. I have never had enough storage space. My first apartment, shared with a good friend from college, was on the ground floor of a small six-story building. It was designated a garden apartment because it was off the back and had a nice little terraced area that functioned like another room five months out of the year. Unfortunately, there were no extra closets out there. When my roommate left, I moved to a studio of my own upstairs where there was one small closet. It seemed like heaven. When I moved a few blocks away to a five-floor walk-up, I had a walk-in closet, except it was called a bedroom. After Howard and I were married we moved into the two-bedroom apartment we're still in today. It seemed then, before the boys were born, we would never run out of space. Naturally, that changed. Eventually they went away to college, but they brought back more stuff than they left with. For twenty-five years the four of us have struggled for every inch of storage. When we bought the house in the country we thought we had finally achieved space. Then the junking and the junk books took over. Could I get rid of some stuff? Could I junk less? Yes and yes. Would life be worth living? I don't think so. When I passed the Manhattan Mini Storage sign on West 23rd Street about a year ago and it blinked out its message, ORGANIZE YOUR APARTMENT, I read LIFE! I made an appointment to look at a space, and afterward decided to create my own.

Above: A galvanized metal shelf unit (71 by 51 by 18 inches) was mine after offering the winning bid of $50 at the Copake Auction, Copake, New York.
Left: Manhattan Mini Storage on West 23rd Street was my wake-up call to create my own mini storage unit.

When I made the decision to create my own storage unit, there was only one place for it—our barn in the country. I decided to claim a space about 16 by 10 feet. (That would cost you about $400 a month in New York City.) I had checked out the interiors of several in-town facilities and each was lined with standard galvanized ridged siding. My son Carter and I headed our pickup north to a local supply yard where we purchased five 12 by 3½-foot galvanized panels. We fitted the panels one over another and nailed them into the old wooden siding. We left a beam showing at either end, which also helped tie in the old plank floors. We are not carpenters, but here's what we learned . . .

storage house rules

- You should not attempt this job by yourself.

- Wear sturdy work gloves when handling the galvanized panels. They are wobbly and have very sharp edges.

- Put the first panel in place up against the wall. You or your partner should be supporting the top of the panel, standing on a reliable ladder. (Forget those junky ones you may have collected for show.) Hammer from the top down. We used 2-inch galvanized roofing nails.

- Fit the outer groove of the next panel over the outer groove of the one you just attached. This gives your wall a seamless appearance.

- Don't get frustrated if you are paneling an old structure. Carter and I could not line up the panels perfectly with the floor. Old buildings are not level!

A collection of eighteen small storage containers—toolboxes, lockboxes, and tackle boxes stacked and organized on the shelves of a galvanized shelf system in my self-made not-so-mini storage space.

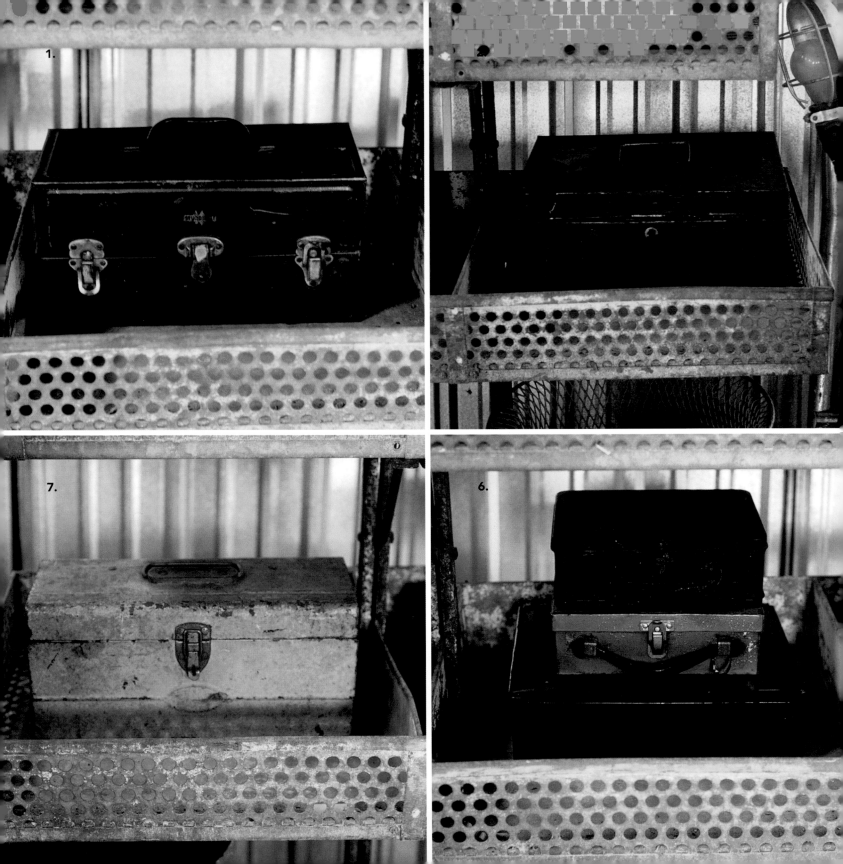

Clockwise from top left: 1. A dark racing green toolbox with a name to give the buyer confidence—STURDIEST—stamped on the front, was $5 at a yard sale. **2.** A classic black metal lockbox. If you're lucky you might find old deeds, wills, locks of hair, or a yellowing stack of love letters inside. I didn't, but paid only $2 at Villa's Antique Auction in Canaan, New York. **3.** I love the simple design of old galvanized trash cans. The one on the right is some kind of liner. These were $5 and $3 at Copake Auction's annual Memorial Day sale, Copake, New York. **4.** An aluminum folding ladder with a top pail shelf. Randy Saunders found a way to use one similar for displaying votive candles; see page 77 for a hint of it. **5.** An old blue-painted industrial wastebasket with a rusted-out bottom. One day I'll replace the bottom so it's functional, but until then I keep it empty and enjoy the shape. It was $1 at Villa's. **6.** A triple stack of storage featuring two lunch boxes: on top, a Fifties classic painted black; the green one below is much older, made of tin with a leather handle. "Joan E. Keller," the name crudely handwritten on the front, must have carried a lot of peanut butter and jelly sandwiches in it. I picked it up on eBay for $12, from a great site maintained by Lisa Durfee at Durflink. Under it is a black tin storage box that is just the right size for old snapshots, maps, and postcards. It was $2.50 on a tag sale table. **7.** I bought this tackle box just for its washy green watercolor look. And I store some small watercolors and bushes inside.

Above: My locker, a $20 find, filled to the brim with the toys of big business: cash register banks and games of chance.
Right: An old metal pushcart, painted fire engine red, was an invaluable aid to any number of unknown factory workers. It served its time at American Junk, our store in White Stone, Virginia, for almost three years before we closed down. Since then I've put it to work, not only toting heavy cargo in my storage unit but as a cool industrial storage unit for my endless supply of magazines and books.

The next step up from storage boxes is lockers, those vertical storage units redolent of high school trysts and the smell of old sneakers. Perhaps because I never had one, I think I have been subconsciously seeking one out. My sister Nell and I found the pair seen above and opposite when we were outside of Richmond, Virginia, looking for new/old merchandise for our American Junk store. We paid about $20 each and dragged them down two flights to our waiting truck. We set them up in our shop to sell, while I secretly prayed that no one would want them. In my heart I knew I had found my elusive locker.

The locker I had longed for in high school has become a toy chest for my big-business high jinks and junk. It's filled with toy cash registers, gaming chips and cards, and, on the bottom shelf, a frame studded with real pennies. It's a genre of Big City collectibles I have dubbed "Money, Money," after the black-hearted ditty in the musical *Cabaret*.

Left: The pale green lockers measure 66 by 18 inches, with shelves a foot deep. The yellow plaid shelf paper they were lined with led me to believe they might have been food pantries in a Fifties kitchen.
Below left: A nut dispenser manufactured in Los Angeles by the Acorn Company. I bought it for more than 5¢ at Junk-a-tique in Millerton, New York. I just loved the little acorn embossed on the dispenser flap.
Below right: A metal cent sign picked up at the Grand Bazaar flea market, New York City, for $15. It was manufactured by the Adler Silhouette Letter Co. and was probably used for some kind of display.

Above: The Fifties oil drum, decorated with the flying red horse of Mobil Oil, didn't stay long in my storage house exhibit. It now serves as a bedside table in my son Carter's studio apartment. It was love at first sight at a tag sale in upstate New York for $5. As for the National Broach & Machine Co. tin, found at the very same tag sale, I was swept away by its strong red-and-black graphics and its illustration of the gear (or is it a broach?) in the center. Oh, and yes, by the price—$1. I use it now to store more romantic tools, a supply of votive candles.

Left: My locker set (each one measures 6 by 1 foot) hauled out of the yard at Hoffman's Barn, Red Hook, New York, for $20.

When it comes right down to it, there are no rules in my storage house. After I salvaged these three school lockers from the old barn store where I found them rusting outside, I decided to take some artistic license with them. Going through a stack of old art magazines I had recently paid 10¢ a copy for, I found some incredible reproductions of Georgia O'Keeffe's flower paintings. I carefully cut out three, and instead of attaching them inside the locker, the way kids use to attach pictures of their heroes and pinup girls, I attached my hero's work on the outside.

139

The Lynn flea market, on the outskirts of Boston — a little bit of everything. Go because you never know.

Suzette Sundae and Dottie strike a pose.

Vintage clothing at Bobby's of Boston.

Secondhand treasures spill onto the sidewalk at Rentparty in Cambridge.

Uniform cool at Bobby's.

Suzette Sundae's — a hot spot for vintage fashion and the finishing touches.

The eternal message of plastic!

Telling time '50s style at Suzette Sundae's.

The real Bobby of Boston at

Take a junk break at Bartley's, a landmark eatery in Cambridge since 1960. It's a feast for the eyes.

Light up your life at Suzette's.

Thrift shop art at the Hadassah, $4 each.

Junk emporium Justin Tyme in Cambridge.

I picked up the hat and the

fleaing boston

There are pockets of great junking spread out all over the Boston area, mostly confined to unique

Kitsch is the catch at Suzette Sundae's in the Allston area of Boston.

Justin Tyme in cozy Cambridge digs.

Furry bow ties, $4, from Home-boy Antiques.

Lush Life's transport parked not far from its Allston storefront, crammed with lush stuff.

the Mayfair Market.

Rentparty's license-plate letters.

A brand I relate to at Bobby's.

Eclectic furniture upstairs at the Hadassah Bargain Spot.

Snapping at a big-city thrift.

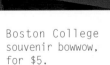

foam finger for just $1 each.

The Collector in Allston: a digger's delight.

Got the thermos for $3.

Boston College souvenir bowwow, for $5.

A sidewalk mural dedicated to the people of Roxbury, spotted on Malcolm X Boulevard.

shops rather than flea markets. For scholarly junking, try Cambridge. For funk, check out Allston and Brighton. Don't miss the best vintage clothing shop, Bobby's of Boston.

WILD AT HEART

Bobby Furst admits to at least a thirty-year garage sale compulsion. He was earlier motivated by an appreciation for old things, and by the need to keep a budget for clothing and household items. Over the last decade his art has fueled his obsession—and vice versa. Today he is constantly on the prowl for weird detritus to feed his off- and on-the-wall assemblages. His entire house, a bungalow built in Laurel Canyon in Los Angeles in 1947, seems to be an assemblage of his own imagination. He moved in ten years ago and before too long, like a child who takes a clock apart to see how it works, he had taken his house apart and put it back together. This renovation took him five and a half years. When it was finished (if it ever is!), he started to fill it up with the booty of his countless garage sale safaris.

Clockwise from top left: 1. The two leopard-skin lounges that dominate Bobby's living room were found separately. The one on the left was just an interesting-shaped frame that he picked up for $10 from a thrift shop in the San Fernando Valley. The other he found at a swap meet years later for $15. He hunted down the menagerie of faux animal print fabrics that cover them and all the pillows throughout the house at various flea markets. Remnants were 25¢ to $1 each. **2.** The hand-carved wooden artist's model is from the turn of the century; Bobby picked it up at a flea market in Reading, Pennsylvania. It was $200! The pink crocheted baby bottle nipple pillow was $15 at a garage sale in Covina, California. **3.** Bobby's version of a mounted antlered animal head, made out of an old bike seat and handlebars. **4.** The large Greek or Roman bath scene was priced at $250 ten years ago at a thrift store in Mar Vista. Signed by Dale in 1967, it was probably made for a movie production. The Tiffany-style lamp was found by Bobby's father in Laguna Beach in the early Sixties. **5.** The "No Pressure" man was created by Bobby out of armchair springs and remnants from an office desk. The chattering teeth came without a key, so they are appropriately chatterless. The eyeballs are from a collection of a dozen pairs that he discovered while walking through the Long Beach flea market. **6.** He filled the goggled glass head with hundreds of keys, and calls it "My Guru." The base is an upside-down chrome bowl from the Eighties. The little hoop man made of bent and twisted wire was a swap meet find. It makes a life statement to Bobby about jumping through hoops.

Previous pages: Right inside Bobby's front door you are greeted by a rather bizarre welcoming committee. At far left is a cloud-covered mannequin he picked up at a garage sale for $5 and slowly transformed into a peace & love child decorated with beads, a peace pin, and a starlike cast-aluminum soil aerator in his hand. On the wall to the left hangs an assemblage of ceramic and clay pieces he collected for about $20 six years ago. The lantern of chunky colored glass in front of it is one of three or four he has discovered at swap meets and thrift stores over the years, ranging in price from $4 to $65. The carved ivory Oriental gentleman to the right of the TV is actually an Italian composite piece picked up at a garage sale for $10. The assemblage behind it is one of Bobby's, partially covered with veneer and with felt stripped from an old upright piano. The circular pieces are actually spring hinges from a double-hung window frame. Next to it on top of the TV is a Picassoesque assemblage by Bobby inspired by an old woman he once saw smoking a corncob pipe in a nearby park. Her hair is styled from more of the felt strips salvaged from the old piano. The Mirolike table, hauled from an estate sale fifteen years ago, was crafted of Italian glass tiles by an artist named Brody in the Sixties. The little metal Swedish baking pan is filled with marbles, pushpins, dice, and other tiny things. The sculpture at the far left caught his eye at a swap meet for $15.

Above: A view from Bobby's front door. The floor tiles, made of more than one hundred different kinds of marble and granite, were bought for $1.50 each at a going-out-of-business tile factory. He laid the 500 pieces down in many configurations throughout the house's reconstruction, before he made his final decision. The painting seen at right hangs on the wall under the bike seat trophy.

Right: Fifteen years ago, Bobby Furst was scouring the newspaper for estate sales when he came upon one in the Los Feliz area that sounded really good. He followed his hunch to a 4,000-square-foot house packed with art. He focused on the cityscape seen at right, gouged, chiseled, and painted out of a piece of linoleum from a battleship. When he tried to talk the price down from $200, the owner told him it was created by a New York artist named Arman, and pointed to his name lit up on a red sign on the painting's far left. Bobby paid the $200. Browsing through a local bookstore years later, he came upon a book on the assemblages of Arman which showed the artist's name spelled out vertically like the sign on the painting. Bobby was thrilled to think his painting might actually be valuable. However, it was very difficult to prove, and after a while he put it back on his wall and decided to just enjoy it. Maybe one day the real story of this daring nightscape of the skyline of New York will be told. Arman, where are you?

Above: Protecting the foot of Bobby's bed are a pair of stunted Moroccan chairs picked up at a garage sale for $5 each. They're piled with a bunch of faux animal skin pillows made from the 25¢ remnants he has collected for years.
Right: Bobby repainted his Forties louvered shade a deep crimson and made a whole new base for it.

Bobby's bedroom, snuggled under the timbered roofline of his one-and-a-half-story bungalow, feels like a cross between an English hayloft and a safari tent. The lamp to the left of his bed, seen above and at right, it is a total assemblage in the Bobby Furst tradition. The red louvered Chinese-styled shade, the kind associated with black panther lamps of the Forties, was attached to a lamp of little significance, priced at $100. He discarded that base and created a new one from a thin wire hourglass-shaped sculpture that became a cage for a dangling crucifix. Attached to the finial on top is a little pewter Jesus. Clip-on earrings and a magical array of dangling odds and ends were added at whim, although not without significance.

I think Isak Dinesen, the famed Danish author of *Out of Africa*, would have enjoyed an afternoon tea with Bobby Furst. She might have seen in him a little of one of her good friends, Denys Finch-Hatton, a hunter of a different sort of wild game. She would have had a keen respect for Bobby's many trophies tracked and hunted down through his years of junking safaris. And she would have been particularly pleased, I think, when she reached the top of the stairs to his bedroom retreat and surveyed the southern sun washing in over leopard-skin rugs and African antlered heads mounted at each corner of the room. Bobby was actually thinking of another heroine, Georgia O'Keeffe, when he mounted these and the one on the exterior of his house, seen on page 151.

Left: With their backs to the sun, two wooden warriors stand watch over Bobby's wardrobe. Though he is certain they were created by the same artist (each is initialed "AM"), he actually discovered them in two different parts of Los Angeles. The taller one was $40, its little brother $25. Over the course of time Bobby has costumed them with disparate finds. He brought the dangling leg, a woman's prosthesis, home from a trip to the Pasadena flea market. It proved to be homemade and quite delicate, a piece of functional art. The African antlered animal, one of four mounted and displayed in the room, was captured at Abel's Auction House in Los Angeles. The white cross, lit with red, white, and blue Christmas lights (Bobby's touch), was found in Reading, Pennsylvania, for about $25. He recently came across a photograph of one similar to it on the podium of a Klu Klux Klan meeting. He hopes his Christmas lights may have exorcised the cross's uncertain past.

Above: Bobby's home sweet home from the east, looking west. Note the homage to O'Keeffe: the steer skull at the peak of the roof was a $20 investment from a garage sale. Its eye sockets have been home over the years to many nesting birds. Peer carefully and you may spot a wild-looking sentry seated on a chair to the right of the balcony seen opposite. This is Bobby's city scarecrow, warding off evil spirits and the like. The 8 by 16-foot trailer is a temporary art studio and shelter for tools and materials until the next project—a permanent studio and carport—begins.

Left: Bobby's mission for artistic meaning doesn't stop at his back door. Walk outside the door of his bedroom and you'll confront one of his most significant collaborations. The welded wonder began when he and a friend were hiking up a trail in Topanga Canyon. They came upon a pile of charred and rusty tools—leftovers from a burned-out garage destroyed by a huge fire that had run through the canyon only weeks before. Bobby filled his pockets, backpack, and a 5-gallon paint can with nails, screws, hammerheads, gears, and faucet handles. Out of those remains came the graceful walkway railing just outside his bedroom door. They were welded together by a friend, the artist Phil Miller. The curving ropy metal that holds the stray artifacts is rebars, the flexible metal rods that are used to strengthen concrete work.

151

Hello, from Hollywood.

At the Melrose Trading Post, held every Sunday, the quintessential L.A. junk, movie posters.

Medical stool, $15, at Melrose.

If you miss the weekend flea markets, Haywire in Hollywood is a well-priced alternative.

A mosaic of souvenir ashtrays spread out at the Melrose Trading Post, each one $3.

Star-quality vintage frames, from $2 up!

The streets of L.A. are lined with tables brimming with junker's gold!

Elvis pillow, $12, at Haywire.

Celeb junk: an Elvis effigy, $1.

On Melrose, a sidewalk star for "Nobody." A tongue-in-cheek message to Hollywood?

Melrose Trading Post, Sundays at Fairfax H.S.

Out of the Closet on Fairfax, one of 14 thrift shops in the L.A. area benefiting AIDS Healthcare.

fleaing los angeles

Whether you rummage through the famous four fleas in Pasadena, Santa Monica, Long Beach, and the Rose

Flotsam and jetsam spilled out of drawers, and out of doors, at one of Liz's Antique Hardware sales.

Beverly Hills Hotel hat, $2, Out of the Closet.

The tented back room at the Community Thrift Store on Fairfax Avenue, one of many to hunt.

Buzz by Busy Bee Hardware.

Academy Awards beauties.

Along Fairfax Avenue there's a great run of thrift shops, many of them housed in Deco buildings.

In the back lot at Bountiful, in Venice.

Drawer pulls, vintage lamp fixtures, porcelain knobs — it's all at Liz's Hardware on La Brea.

Four great flea markets rotate locations every Sunday of the month. See the Junk Guide, page 231.

Thrift shop fifis of L.A., 50¢ each.

Your own hot dog stand in the outdoor lot at The Sanctuary — seems more New York than Los Angeles.

A shrine to Junk — The Sanctuary.

Bowl, visit the thrifts on Fairfax, go "alleying" (see page 128), or even hit the local recycling yard, L.A. gets an Academy Award for star-quality junk resources!

153

URBAN ARCHAEOLOGY

John Bennett traveled to the French countryside almost thirty years ago to paint the picturesque scenery. But lying on a grassy hill in Brittany he stretched out his arms and touched something that in turn touched his life and art in an irrevocable way. What he felt was the rough edge of an ancient axhead that had been buried for hundreds of years. He carefully dug it up and fell in love with its shape and color, its rustiness, and the unknown story that clung to it like the earth that had held it for so long. Eventually, the axhead returned with him to New York City and inspired his quest for other orphaned fragments abandoned in the streets and sidewalks of his urban neighborhood. He takes them home, cleans them up, and lives with them in his studio on the first floor of the pre–Civil War building he and his wife Karen bought twenty-three years ago. When the time seems right, he takes a piece upstairs to their main living space and adds it to one of the collections displayed on the shelves that line the room, seen opposite. The collection today totals about one hundred artifacts, which seems spare considering his three-decade search. But it isn't when you consider the qualities he demands from his pieces. It must have a past with a story to tell, like the mashed muffler on the opposite page, top left. Each must have survived some life-threatening ordeal. In the end he sees the poetry that moved him, not long after his discovery in France, to start sculpting. He hopes that his own handmade pieces feel as aged and mysterious as the born-again spoils of his urban digs, and that axhead recovered so long ago from out of the earth.

Above: One of John Bennett's sculptures, a 12-inch-tall concrete figure balanced on a tightrope on a table in his New York City studio.
Far left, top to bottom: 1. A fossilized muffler looking like a Cubist painting was found on the West Side Highway. Beside it, a beat-up piece of copper piping. **2.** A squared-off number 8 leads a lineup of bent and rusted metal sticks. The deformed square piece among them was cut by a blowtorch. Why? For what purpose? **3.** From the animal collection, a turtle with its head up and a cat with ears, eyes, and a mouth (seen again on the lower shelf at right). **4.** To the left and below, one of John's sculpted masks, a found piece that looks like the head of a cobra.
Left: Thin strips of metal and wood support a variety of orphaned objects on a wall opposite John and Karen's dining area. The lowest shelf supports a train of small animal-like fragments. On the middle shelf, from the left, John sees a frog, cat, and tortoise, creating a small and more abstract commingling. Above left, what appears to be a bucket handle is rippled as if it were handmade by the likes of a Giacometti. The curved piece to the upper right looks, to John, like a herring's head.

Every day for the first seven days after the Bennett's German shepherd Lamont died, John sculpted a little concrete mask in his memory. He lined them up sequentially on a ledge in the living room to keep Lamont's presence nearby. Above the ledge he placed a 30-inch-long steel plate embossed with a symmetrical leaf pattern. His theory is that someone used a welding torch to cut this imperfect piece out of a larger sheet, most often seen as flooring for loading docks. Why? Possibly to tighten something in the back of a truck? He loved the perfect leaf pattern within the imperfectly cut edges, and the idea that someone had created it out of an already functioning element. The hefty piece guarding the end of the seven masks is a 15 by 4-inch piece of steel plate with straight vertical sides and an uneven top and bottom resulting from a blowtorch operation.

Far right: The New York City water pipe, a solid yet battered pedestal for one of John's concrete figures, was rescued from a dig right outside the Bennetts' front door. City workers making repairs hauled out the mighty receptacle (circa 1930) and left it in a pile to be taken away. John got there first with his sturdy handtruck. It was the catch of the day, measuring 3 feet of solid cast iron. Behind it are a lineup of larger masks.

Right: The centerpiece of John's collection lives on new pine shelves lodged between a set of bookshelves and the kitchen cabinets. On top of it floats what looks like a sailboat but is in fact a sail-shaped piece of white enamel. The wrench, seen on the second shelf from the bottom, eaten away by age and rust, was found in an old box of tools left in their building. The washers, like rusty doughnuts in all different sizes, are no longer manufactured.

In an article in *The New York Times* on January 22, 2000, Laurence Zuckerman reports that "in prehistoric caves dating back to 40,000 years, archaeologists have discovered strange curios, including shells and oddly shaped lumps of iron pyrite. They are, the scientists believe, the first evidence of the human impulse to collect." John Bennett saw the article and e-mailed me this quote with a postscript which read, "This gave me goose bumps when I read it. It's me." Looking at the strange curios he has placed so systematically on the simple wooden shelves near the family kitchen, I thought he may be right. Close scrutiny reveals a wrench, on the second shelf from the bottom, and a series of worn-out washers, but most of the objects are unidentifiable and made of iron, though not iron pyrite! The article goes on to examine the impulse to collect. Susan M. Pearce, a professor at the University of Leicester in England, who has done research on collecting, said in an interview, "If 33 percent of people are doing it, you can't really call it peculiar. These people have cars, children, homes. They all live normal lives. It's not a symptom of weirdness or deviance."

Like John Bennett, Christoper Bailey and David Horowitz are dedicated to the preservation of urban fossils. Unlike John, their sights are set on one endangered species, the manhole covers in New York City. As cities repave their sidewalks and streets, these historic openings to the underground are fast disappearing. But not if David and Christopher have anything to do with it. To date they have made over 120 plaster impressions (see a few at left) right from the street. The oldest cover, dated 1873, was discovered on Duane Street in lower Manhattan. Not only do the two save the artistic designs, but they also add the street detritus that makes them authentic. After casting the forms in plaster, Christopher and David sprinkle on shattered windshield glass, nails, gravel, and dirt. They're my kind of cooks!

ROOM
AT THE TOP OF THE STAIRS

I have never met Fritzie. A long-distance introduction by a mutual friend and collector led to endless back-and-forth calls from New York, my Big City, to her Big City, San Francisco. Our conversations evolved into a telephone miniseries that traced her journey from a high bluff in Burlington, Iowa, where she was born and baptized Pamela Fritz, to a hill in San Francisco, where she has dedicated seven years to restoring an 1888 Victorian jewel of a house (see the entrance on the opposite page, far right). When I finally stood at the bottom of her black-and-white stairway, it was like walking into the pages of a favorite novel, except the mysterious heroine was not at home. Fritzie was off again, foraging for treasures for Interieur Perdu, her incredible shop tucked under the spans of the Bay Bridge (for a sneak peek, turn to page 234). Follow me up the stairs and fall in love with two floors of modern romance—Fritzie's heartwarming Big City style.

Above: Fritizie's house is divided three ways with three front doors. Hers is just out of sight to the far right.

Left: In a corner of her work studio, a styling moment right out of *Great Expectations* sans the spiderwebs. The misty white curtains were swept up from a dealer's stall at her favorite L'Isle-sur-la-Sorgue flea market in Provence, France. The bistro chair and table from Interieur Perdu (her warehouse shop of lost and found French treasures) would cost you about $65 and $275, respectively. A Fritzie way to display a chandelier: don't hang it, lean it on a table, along with a couple of chunky melting candles. The lounge chair glimpsed at the foot of the curtains is covered by convent sheets (see more on her bed, page 175), stocked at Interieurs Perdu for around $65.

Opposite: After an excruciating removal of brown shag carpeting from the old wooden stairway just inside her leaf-green front door, Fritzie created a faux runner with shiny black paint.

161

The "farm-girl/glamour-puss" that Fritzie describes herself as doesn't quite account for the poetry of the black-and-white photographs found on walls, up staircases, stuck into mirrors, and piled into boxes and baskets throughout her house. She does not coddle her collections, she lives with them. Her "anti-frames" (seen opposite and at left) exemplify that spirit and possibly go back to the values of simple living she learned growing up back in a small town in Iowa.

Opposite, far left: Just as she bares her photographs by clamping them to the wall unframed, Fritzie bares other things too, like this skinny black lamppost. "It came into Perdu and I had to have it!" She converted it and screwed in a beautiful little beaded light bulb (from Nest, on Fillmore, for $24). Without a shade it becomes a light in the darkness.
Opposite, left: Her name Is Hazel and though Fritzie has never met her she lives throughout the house in photographs by her friend Eva Seay. This one hangs on the stairway to the second floor, secured by a simple office clamp. "I love it so abstract and pure," sighs Fritzie, "and the way the edges curl. No frame. It's free, like Hazel."
Left: Enter Fritzie's bedroom and you are struck with the ying/yang of black and white, bold and sensitive. Another Hazel image, this time caught in an old ghost town with a friend named April. Fritzie brought the chandelier back from Privy, her favorite antique shop in Burlingame, Iowa, for $35. She had it rewired and added the Fritzie touch: a little crystal ball she dug out of a box at a flea market in Paris and dangled on the base.

163

These pages, from above to right: Jasper, Fritzie's chocolate Labrador retriever, resting on a pair of straw pillows on the living room sofa. Fritzie's black-and-white look in one of her two living rooms. The pair of mostly black "spring" garden chairs were collected from Zonal, a San Francisco landmark shop of eclectic style, for $50 seven years ago. The sconce above is one of a pair that were $40, from Gravy Boat Antiques, Sacramento. They were leftover display pieces ("not very old—probably from the Fifties or Sixties") salvaged by our style goddess. The large white mirror, on the other hand, is old, turn of the century, and found on a French foraging trip. "I painted it white because it was really beat up, but mostly because I prefer mirrors not to stand out. I like them to reflect other objects in the space." The folding bistro table it rests on supports, among other things, her black pointy glasses, pharmacy measures filled with wooden and ceramic eggs (from Privy Antiques, Burlingame, Iowa, $5 each), an 18th-century Georgian glass absinthe measure, 19th-century bell jars filled with hyacinth bulbs, an aluminum army medical box for storing old surgical tools, and a white funeral vase. A fuller view of the "spring chair," seen opposite, reveals more missing paint. "It's not a chair people rush to sit in," chuckles Fritzie, which is just fine since she bought it primarily for its graphic quality. Fritzie's mirror at work, reflecting a still life of sun-drenched sap buckets, drooping long-stemmed tulips, and Jasper's heroic profile.

When a painter friend told her about the amazing Victorian house circa 1888, complete with bay windows and gingerbread trim, that was for sale across the street from him, she went to take a look. Somehow she saw beyond the sixteen broken windows, the brown shag carpet, the filth, and the mess. It is helpful to know that in the years between the farm in Iowa and Interieur Perdu (launched with two friends five years ago), Fritzie traveled to Dallas for a quick stint with Great-aunt Geraldine. "Though I adored her daisy sandals, false eyelashes, and piled-up hair, I hated flashy Dallas." Los Angeles was the next stop, where she landed a job in travel marketing, but yearned for "creativity." Fritzie hooked up with a display team at Saks and eventually caught the eye of the I. Magnin group, which made her visual director of their Sacramento store. Three years later she was named head visual director and stylist of their flagship store in San Francisco. Then a trip to Paris brought her the inspiration for her ultimate creative experience—LuLu Wireworks. "I had seen some incredibly beautiful display furniture made of wire and decided to mimic it in miniature," she explained. It was about this time that the house came into her life. Not only was it a stylist's dream—or nightmare—but it was a close replica of the Victorian houses in that childhood town in Iowa she had left so long ago.

Color in Fritzie's black-and-white palace! Nine oddly sized and spaced sap buckets washed in pastel tints and nailed onto the living room wall look like silos without their tops. "I love black and white but I like it spiked with shots of color. A strict diet of black and white would be boring," says Fritzie. Glowing in the late afternoon sun that streams through her big bay window, the buckets create a 3-D watercolor. At night, light streams out of them from the chunky votives placed inside. She notes they create a kind of angel light, "that ethereal kind of glow." Instead of placing the tulips in the sap buckets, as most people would, she cages them inside a French street trash basket, $150 at Perdu. Once again she has transformed simple worker tools into born-again objects of her very personal imagination.

Carson McCullers would have swooned over the clock, 5 feet in diameter, that hangs like a giant blue wristwatch to the right of the sap buckets, seen on the preceding pages. It was Fritzie's version of the Clock Without Hands when she confronted it in Normandy. It and two others had been removed from a demolished church. Since then, the hands have been replaced with a rusty orange pair. It's all window dressing, just another big prop in her life, since the clock doesn't work. "That's what I really like about it—a clock so big and so useless, that doesn't tell time." Yet the hands are movable, so she can make it any time she wants it to be. The cost? Priceless, but if you must know—$2,400 wholesale. Imagine if it worked!

Clockwise from the top left: 1. If you go back to the sofa Jasper chose to rest on (page 164), you'll know exactly where this coffee table lives: right in front of it. Fritzie dragged it home from a flea market for $250. Placed carefully on top is a pair of numbers—a 5 and an 8—picked out of a tray of numbers in an old printing shop in France. They were $15 each. Above them, a little box from Holland supports three votive candles. The kumquats are placed in a shallow container made for funeral floral arrangements. **2.** How unusual is it to find a 7-foot table in your favorite color? Not only did Fritzie find a long table—in orange—but she found it in the basement of her very own house—free! The double lamp base she found at a garage sale in Stinson Beach for $5. She took it to Light Opera, wizards of old lamp restoration (see Junk Guide, page 234), and topped it with a pair of perfect parchment shades from the Thirties at Tribeca, Burlingame, California. The array of bistro chairs in green and orange fold up for easy storage and portability. You can find them at Fritzie's store, Interieur Perdu, for $65, or hunt around for American knock-offs—they're everywhere. **3.** Fritzie's love for magazines started when her grandparents loaded her down with stacks of old *Vogues* tied up in string. Today she keeps her new collection in old army supply bins from the Forties. Look for something similar in well-stocked army navy stores, at flea markets, or these French army versions at Interieur Perdu, for $65. **4.** A pulled-back perspective of the sun-flooded living room reveals the true scale of Fritzie's salvaged timepiece.

home work

Whatever drives it—ambition, power, excitement, sex, money, love, inspiration, challenge—in the end, the Big City engine is WORK! It's what causes people to leave small towns—like Pamela Fritz, Randy Saunders, and Jereny Blas, who moved to San Francisco (see page 76), Mark Clay to Dallas (see page 105), and Anita Calero and Don Freeman to New York (pages 199 and 91). Or it's what makes those who were born there, stay—like my son Carter in New York (see page 20) or Bobby Furst in Los Angeles (see page 143). Whether they work in an office or their office is a cell phone and a car, or a photo studio, or a laptop on a plane, most Big City workers bring home work.

Left: Fritzie's home studio, seen on the next four pages, is punctuated by still lifes of things that inspire her, like this little lineup poised on top of an enamel-topped surgical cart from the Twenties. Starting at the left, a bowl contains family photographs, but not of Fritzie's family. She has treasured the straw-stuffed mannequin's head, circa 1920, since her store display days, when she found it at the Pasadena flea market in Los Angeles. Every home office needs a clock; Fritzie, as you may recall, prefers hers with no hands. She recovered this one from France at the same time she got its jumbo cousin, seen on page 168. In front of the wooden toolbox (Interieur Perdu, $75) rests an old croquet ball ("for the shape"), and on top of it stands a cardboard pop-up Eiffel Tower, in honor of the fact, says Fritzie, that "after ten years of trips to France and Paris, I finally made the ascent!"

The norms of a home office don't quite fit Fritzie's work studio. But wait, is that a file cabinet yonder, at right, standing duty on what appears to be a worktable? Fritzie confirms it is indeed, and that each of the twelve little drawers secures some form of office item, including paper clips, small yellow pencils, erasers, rubber bands, clamps, staples, and the like. The little brass pulls have long since turned green and the nameplates no longer identify what's inside, but that's just fine with Fritzie. She snagged it at a French flea market for $20. A black-and-white vase by Jonathan Adler, a New York artist, sits on top of the cabinet. The little wire In box, designed for silverware and napkins, stores photographs, with one of her parents' wedding portraits on top. The box was brought back from a visit home from Privy Antiques for $10. The bona fide desk lamp overlooks a large, official-looking calendar.

An artistic jumble of souvenirs and supplies is stored on a mobile cart just to the left of Fritzie's worktable. It's actually a surgical cart from the Twenties, laid out with two large enamel shelves with space below for some newer, expandable files. It was her prized find at San Francisco's huge annual flower show. It took a lot of talking (plus $500!) to evict thirty pots of plants from their happy home. Fritzie's own flower show is in constant bloom, thanks to the box full of vintage corsages she unearthed in the basement of an old residential hotel she once lived in in downtown San Francisco. They're attached to a pair of equally vintage bust forms, souvenirs of the Chanel accessory boutique at I. Magnin, her old styling/stomping ground in the late Eighties. The second shelf is crammed with a variety of storage wire and metal baskets. The one in the middle that resembles a cheese grater is one of several locker baskets she gathered up for $15 each at an outdoor junkyard under the freeway in Oakland. (I've seen them for less at a number of flea markets, most recently at the Lakewood flea market in Atlanta—see page 206.)

Opposite, left: A more corporate look is supplied by the serious aluminum desk chair, circa 1940, one of a pair Fritzie purchased for $75 each at Zonal. The childish graffiti carved into the 5½-foot-long table reveals its past as a school table. The big mirror, another example of her love of the large, supports and contrasts with the tiny images framed above.

Fritzie's bedroom, seen on these two pages, is the room at the top. When the building was divided up into three flats with three different entrances, she got the top two floors. The light pours from the original windows to the south and from skylights added in the Seventies. It is her haven, furnished sparely with a few favorite objects, including giant numbers and tiny leopard-skin prints.

Clockwise from right: 1. "I saw the leopard-skin chair and a mate in the window of a junk shop in Sacramento. They were so Fifties whacky that they fit my personality perfectly," reports Fritzie. She paid $125 for them more than ten years ago, and finds they still work today, especially as a resting place for her favorite mock-croc bag and leopard-skin gloves. The gloves were a gift, the bag, $5 after she had dug it out of the mud under a vendor's table at a flea market in Sausalito. **2.** The purity of Fritzie's bed, covered in a large French convent sheet, is slightly disturbed by a trio of animal-print throw pillows, leftovers from her I. Magnin stylist days. The number 2, an old gas station graphic circa 1960, is one of a collection that she displays in different places throughout her home. It was $20 from Zonal. **3.** Her initials, PF, in zinc were a gift from Bill from his store, Aria. Above them is a wrinkled brown paper envelope made and sent by her artist friend Kimberly Austin. **4.** In a spare room down the hall, a velvet leopard-skin satchel hangs next to an expandable wire torso from the late Twenties. The mannequin form (another French find) works on its own as an airy piece of sculpture or as a 3-D bulletin board for collections of postcards, paper flowers, photographs, even a handmade envelope. **5.** A little side glass and metal table from Zonal—one of a pair that cost $50. The Lucite lamp, circa the groovy Sixties, was a Folsom Street find, $50, from a funky shop in Sacramento. A gas station number 3 billboards the wall behind it. **6.** The miniature vanity stool is the first archival piece created for Lulu's Wireworks, Fritzie's line of miniature wire works of art. The red rose was from the box of vintage blooms Fritzie uncovered years back in a basement.

1.

3.
TO: Intérieurs Perdu
340 Bryant Street
San Francisco, CA.
94107

STARVING ARTIST

When I was about fifteen years old, I had a recurring dream about coming to New York City and moving into a very bohemian space in Greenwich Village. Obviously, I'm dating myself since no starving artist could afford to live in the Village today. Many have moved across the Williamsburg Bridge to different parts of Brooklyn, although it just doesn't sound as romantic. I did make it to New York City, but never lived in the Village. I knew a few artists, but most of them were doing pretty well, and none had the fantasy loft I had dreamed of. Last year I decided to cheat reality and create my own—not in Greenwich Village, but in our barn loft in upstate New York. Of course, I'm not a painter or a sculptor, but I could pretend and collect paintings and pottery, brushes, and easels and everything else needed to live out my Big City junk fantasy. And then, when the fantasy lost its luster, I would take down the paintings and the funny palette clock, gather the sculpture, ceramics, paints, and brushes, and take them back to the city to inject a little fantasy into my real life in a real apartment.

Above: A composition of artistic fun on my worktable in my fantasy painter's studio. The stylish artist, a handmade doll, has got to be a French Impressionist. Note his striped T-shirt, his jaunty straw hat, and his chic bandanna ascot. Oh, and check out those orange espadrilles! Although the painting he clutches is a silly portrait of a clown, I hope he can paint as well as he dresses.

Left: Picking art as a theme doesn't limit you to collecting junk master paintings, although these are my favorites, or paintbrushes and easels. On my first tour around a rather large flea market in downtown New York I spotted what at first glance appeared to be a classic artist's palette. When I stepped over for a closer look, I gasped to see it was even better: this was an ingenious conversion of a palette into a clock! I checked out the price—$20—made up my mind to try to get it for less, but knew in my heart I would go for broke on this one. But then (this happens) I couldn't find the dealer. One of her colleagues recognized her across the lot, gave a yell, and I took off in hot pursuit. The dealer agreed to $15 (it was the end of the day), and by the next weekend my purchase was telling real time in my unreal artist's studio!

Artists' studios are not dainty. Some look like a welder's workshop. Creative people who splatter paint, fling clay, and mix large vats of plaster need to surround themselves with utility stools, tables, and bins. They require furniture that is durable, low-maintenance, and mobile.

Above: Artists might prefer to have a sturdier worktable than my circular wooden petal table. On the other hand, they just might approve of it as a display base for their creations, as I did. Plus it has wheels, so it can travel. I begged it off my neighbor Kitty Paris for $25.

Right: Any self-respecting artist would welcome this handy wheeled industrial storage cart into their studio. But think of it alternatively in a kitchen, with butcher block on top, cookbooks below. Or it could be a hefty bedside table for an extra-tall bed, or hold kids' toys and games. In my fantasy life as an artist I use it to store a set of fix-it encyclopedias, $15 at the Rummage Shoppe, Millerton, New York, some sculpting tools, and a book on ceramics. Up top I made a still life of glass grapes and weird pottery. The canvas seat was $5 at the SoHo flea market. The cart, by the way, cost me $10 at a street sale on Canal Street.

I am trying to remember how I got this large canvas of the Blues Sisters, at left, into a taxi and home from the 26th Street flea market—fifty-four blocks away. But I don't let details like that stand in the way of owning something my heart says "yes" to, particularly when the price is right—$10 for the sisters! True, the painting had lost flecks of color and the frame was a little warped, but I prefer works of art that have lived. And as for framing your works of art, if you've read my other junk books, then you know I feel the same way about framing paintings that Pamela Fritz feels about framing photographs. (Her "anti-framing" methods can be appreciated on page 163.) I love the simplicity of frameless oils on painter's board, or framed canvases. Drawings and watercolors present a different challenge. In that case I prefer the simplest dime-store frame, either painted or smeared with gesso.

Left: A green work stool, picked up at a city street tag sale for $10, looks as though the seller might have been a starving artist. The toolboxes, a twin set in blue, were $5 for the pair at the SoHo flea market.

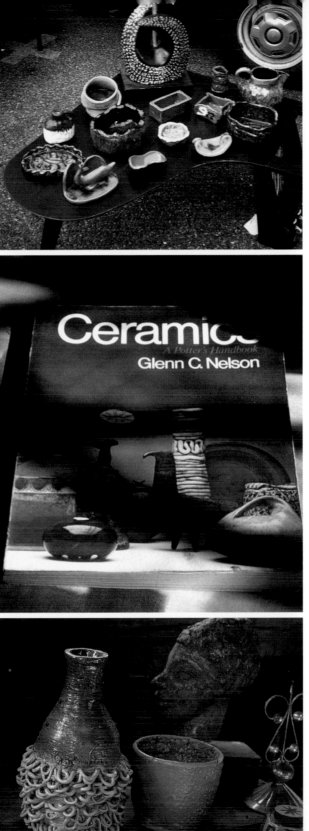

Once again I'm pretending to be something I'm not—a painter, a sculptor, a potter. I always thought shaping a lump of wet clay on a wheel would be so sensual. Until now, however, I've never tried it, but to fill the void I have stockpiled quite a collection of weird pottery, the more primitive the better.

Top: I discovered this collection of hand-crafted ceramics on display at the 26th Street flea market many years ago. I bought the green porpoise at the front far left corner of the table, the rectangular turquoise box in the center, and the pink and green circular piece in front of it for very little; the artist/dealer was thrilled for the appreciation. Those three pieces set me on the weird pottery hunt that I continue today.

Middle: A ceramics book I picked up at a tag sale for $1. Art books are easy prey at most good markets.

Bottom: Oh, to meet the artist whose hands and heart shaped this weirdest of all pots! That would be the green one with the scalloped loops, at the far left. I eyed it for months at the Rummage Shoppe, Millerton, New York, and finally broke down and bought it for $3. I brought back the metal profile of a lady in the overhead bin of a plane from a trip to Los Angeles. It was $12 at the Pasadena flea market. The blue pot was 50¢ at a children's art sale. The silver whatchamacallit is, I think, a beheaded Mexican candlestick holder, resurrected from a box lot of stuff from an auction.

Opposite: Center stage in my fantasy studio is the ceramics exhibit arranged on the top of the petal table. The entire collection was created by a very promising young artist, my niece Cary Hunter Thompson, in a summer project when she was eight. It is on loan from her mother, Nell.

"You are in demand if you can draw! FREE Talent Test Offer INSIDE!" What a tantalizing come-on this was, printed on the Fifties match cover seen in the clamshell ashtray at right and on the opposite page. Paper match packs were the mini-billboards of the era. What better way to get your message right into the hands, literally, of the consumer? After all, everybody smoked: even the artist pictured is smoking a pipe. His model, scantily clad, probably has a cigarette somewhere nearby. Inside the match cover is an offer for a free talent test, with a tiny coupon to fill in and send to Art Instruction, Inc. of Minneapolis. Matchbooks also advertised candy bars, zippers, hotels, restaurants, paints and housewares, banks, insurance companies, lumber, train and airline companies, accountants, congressional candidates, and even a way to receive a high school diploma! I never collected matchbooks until recently when I paid about $30 for an old suitcase filled with at least a hundred of them. Each one is a tiny work of art and commerce. When I came upon the Talent Test offer I was hooked and howling! I may do what a match maniac friend of mine did and upholster both sides of a room screen with matchbook covers.

Right: Perhaps Ethel Pollack, the artist who created this 9 by 12-inch oil on canvas board, signed up for the free at-home talent test offered inside the matchbook below it. Her small masterpiece (a self-portrait?) was exhibited at The Bottle Shop, Washington Hollow, New York, for $1.

Still life: matchbook nestled in a pointillist clamshell ashtray, a tag sale find for 25¢, resting on a six-sided ceramic dish from Italy that was buried in a box of auction booty. I assembled this tableau on an old checkers game board, seen opposite, that cost me less than a dollar.

Above: A child's Chinese pajama top, discovered in the window of Sheppard Street Antiques in Richmond, Virginia, for $45, hangs on a ledge of my studio; it serves as an ornamental prop or an outfit for a child model—if one were to drop in!
Right: The clay sculpture of a seated nude was irresistible when I saw her on a cluttered table at one of the weekend parking lot markets on Sixth Avenue near 26th Street in New York. It is signed by the artist, Soffen, who would have been scandalized that I paid only $5 for it!

Let me guide you through my dream studio, the second of two I have created from my junkmaster journeys. (The first was published in *American Junk*.) This one, set up in the loft of my barn, will eventually be replaced by some other stage set built from junk to satisfy my longing for other, imagined vocations.

Left: I'm not really a leopard-skin kind of chick, but when this pair of chic spotted flats appeared on the lawn at a huge yard sale thrown by my friend Lisa Durfee (be sure to visit her on-line auctions and her booth at The Elephant Trunk Flea Market in New Milford, New York—see Junk Guide, page 233, for specifics), I shopped till I dropped $4 for them! Of course, they're too small for me, but then I had no intention of ever wearing them. They became pointy works of footwear art beside another fashionable find, a wooden checkers box lined with a faux leopard-skin in corduroy. This was hunted down in New York's SoHo flea market, just a stone's throw from the city's hot fashion boutiques, for $5.

Middle: A glass wine decanter tattooed with fantastic painted spots of a psychedelic breed caught at the Antique Bazaar on 25th Street. I think I picked it up the same day I purchased the Blues Sisters, slightly out of focus behind it, and in focus on page 179. I plunked down two dollars for it.

Right: Fantasies make you bravely say yes to things you'd normally only dream of owning. How about the exotic blooming lamp I courageously chose at the Rummage Shoppe, Millerton, New York, for $10? The craziness went further when I topped the bulb with one of those green metal industrial shades, $2 from the Alemany flea market, San Francisco. After alighting the nude above it—a true junk masterpiece, bought from Lisa Durfee for $20—it now lights up my husband Howard's city study. The orange-glazed pitcher next to it was a Fiesta ware knock-off bought so long ago I don't remember where I got it. But I'm sure I didn't spend more than $12 for it. The little green chair with a metal base that secures it to the floor was manufactured by the Kennedy Brothers (any relation?) in Boston, Massachusetts. I picked it up for about $10 in a junk shop yard in upstate New York.

Heralded as the ultimate dig-in junk shop, Betty's was closed down when I finally got there.

My major Chicago find, a cityscape of the downtown circa 1950, from Brooke James.

A $35 storage solution at Salvation Army.

Vintage hangers at Robin Richman's

Illinois sash & peace button, $9.

The Broadway Antique Market, a former car dealership, is now filled with dealers in high-quality junk.

A Chicago Transit sweater, $7, Salvation Army.

Red Eye, one of many junk shops on North Lincoln.

The eyes have it at Danger

There are seven Salvation Army shops in Chicago. This one on North Union has three stories.

Uncle Fun's homage to King Elvis.

At Uncle Fun's: three goofy greeting cards, three plastic toy poodles, and eight fashion plates, for a total of $5.

Pause for used books

fleaing chicago

The Windy City swept me away with its endless avenues lined with one great shop after another. For cool and

boutique on North Damen.

Snapping some Big City inspriation.

From Uncle Fun, another souvenir of downtown Chicago in metal, for only $3.

A toy shop of playthings from our childhoods, like a plastic squirt gun shaped like a fish.

City on West Belmont.

Stop for a bite at the Bongo Room while you peruse the likes of Brooke James and Green Acres on North Milwaukee.

A red cooler and old cooker at Brooke James.

Lisa and Keri, sisters and co-owners of Brooke James, have a romantic eye for mixing junk.

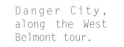

on North Milwaukee.

Danger City, along the West Belmont tour.

Funny Fifties glasses mounted on the facade of a modern eyewear shop caught my eye.

Another detail of my Chicago cityscape, painted by Skokie artist Harry Rubens in the Fifties.

sophisticated junk, go to North Milwaukee. For funky junk at Danger City and Uncle Fun, troop down West Belmont, then head to North Lincoln. A word of advice: don't go in January like I did!

NO VACANCY

Fred Bernstein confesses that his childhood dream was to be a garbageman. He used to rummage through the abandoned goods of his neighborhood in Pittsburgh, until his mother had a fit. "Then she got hooked on thrift shopping," reports Fred with a hint of gleeful revenge. He kept collecting in Pittsburgh, then moved on to Philadelphia, then New York, and ended up filling a spacious three-bedroom house in south Florida with all of his accumulated stuff. Because his work as a stylist ("That's what I do for a living—I shop!") for commercials, ads, and magazines kept him on the road a lot, he decided to sell the house. "I could move anywhere!" For a while he and his Egyptian pharaoh hound Farouk stayed with friends, then in a hotel for three months. And what about all the things that had filled up his house? He didn't ditch them, but instead packed them all away in rented storage space. When the time came to settle, he decided on Miami Beach, where he frequently worked, and there he chose an apartment by the ocean. After signing the lease, he stood in the doorway of his new home and pondered the fact that it was a 460-square-foot studio. He had an anxiety attack, then took a deep breath and decided to turn it into the perfect hotel room. He decided to choose a few of the things he couldn't live without and a few he felt would be serviceable, and then he and Farouk went for a swim in the ocean.

Above: Fred checked into his new home, the Sea Crest Apartments, a resort accommodation built in Miami Beach in the Thirties, in 1999.
Opposite, clockwise from near left: The louvered glass door to Fred's motel home is lined up next to a row of them along the balcony. The welcoming committee, a toy grasshopper and ladybug, were props from a shooting. The folding chair was a $2.50 yard sale find. The gargoyle, one of a pair guarding the entrance, was found for about $20 at an outdoor masonry yard in Miami.

Above: What Fred saw when he stood in the door of his new 460-square-foot home.
Far left: Just inside the studio, resting on a steel-based table covered with walnut veneer, are worker toys left by an architect friend. The lamp, found at the Bargain Barn in Miami, was a $1 find.
Left: Piled with photography books, Fred's footstool ("more of a table, really") was a thrift shop present from a friend. It is covered with a sophisticated checkerboard fabric.

This is how it happens: You are exploring a place called the Bargain Barn in Miami. You happen to see something in a mess of stuff under a table. You gingerly pull it up, don't make a fuss, and pay the $1 the dealer is asking for it. You walk on nonchalantly, half expecting her to shout out, "I've made a mistake, come back!" You make it to the car and discover an incredible lamp, probably from the Fifties. About a year and a half after you purchase it, you're reading a foreign edition of *Elle Décor*, and there it is—your lamp! It's a brand-new version listed for $400. Does it change the way you feel about your $1 treasure? Do you love it any more? Not really.

"What would you want to have with you if you were stranded alone on a desert island?" That old hypothetical question was similar to what Fred faced as he confronted a lifetime of possessions. His new space was an island of sorts. What would he need in less than 500 square feet to make life pleasurable? At the top of that list was a batallion of nine glass and ceramic vases, seen at ease in a corner of his new spartan digs, at right. Why these? Practically, he surmised they wouldn't survive exile in a storage bin. And emotionally, he loves the look of them. Their colors remind him of water, an attraction he has nurtured since he was a boy. "When I didn't feel good I would take a bath," he recalls. These nine vases are soothing like that.

Right: The tall drink of water at the left "was the first thing I picked out for myself when I had made some money." It cost him $75, in a pricey little shop on Manhattan's Upper East Side. The ombréd orange-and-yellow balloonlike vase he brought back from an antique mall in Pittsburgh for $40. He was on the road from New York to Florida when he spotted the antique mall sign that led him to the speckled vase with the odd handle, which he believes is Red Wing. That detour cost him $60. He made up for it at a yard sale in Shelter Island, New York, where he found the lightly glazed Caribbean blue vase for 50¢. The graceful black vase speckled with stripes of watercolors was a gift. The thin smoky glass decanter was another Shelter Island find for $10. The most expensive member of the group is the pumpkin-colored striated piece he found for $125 at a craft fair in Miami. The tall buttery tower of glass behind it was collected for $35, also at that mall in Pittsburgh. And finally, he doesn't have a clue where he bought the dark teal pitcher!

Fred Bernstein's closet is a sea of black and white. He's just more comfortable in colors that don't stand out. It's not surprising, then, that his living quarters are similarly hued. "I'm very color sensitive. Neutral colors—black, white, sepia, beige—are calming." When it comes to scale, he prefers things low to the ground. This works particularly well in his small, low-ceilinged space. The walnut veneer side table, the footstool, even the vases seen on the preceding pages don't rise much above knee level.

Right: How low can Fred go? His reddish-black console rises only about 1½ feet off the floor. At about 5 feet, it is long enough to support his TV, video player, and a few favorite objects. He pulled it out of an avalanche of stuff in the back acre of Douglas Garden Thrift Store—a classic in Miami Beach (see the Junk Guide, page 231) for $65. Each end is anchored with a black football-shaped stereo speaker. The heavy glass ashtray, known as a geode, was found for $10 ("I was shocked it was so cheap") on an overnight job in Savannah. "I always try to carve out time to forage when I'm on a job," Fred says. His much cherished "nun" lamp was a relic of the Meadowlands Flea Market at Giants Stadium, East Rutherford, New Jersey, for $25. The tile floor is covered with a large sisal rug banded in black.

For a man who makes his living creating images, Fred's walls are refreshingly blank. When he gets home from the houses and commercial sets he works in, nothing is probably very refreshing.

Left: Do we discern a splash of color amid a sea of black and white and sepia in Fred's chosen palette of calm colors? (Check out Pamela Fritz on page 164, and you'll find a similar philosophy about spiking black and white with a shot of color.) It's actually an orange glass ceiling shade posing as a diminutive vase on top of one of Fred's sleek black music-system units. It came from one of those mythic yard sales when Fred lived in another shore community, Shelter Island, New York. The photograph above it was a find from the Douglas Garden Thrift Store in Miami Beach, but he doesn't know where it was taken. "It could be a lake in the Adirondacks or one in Italy." What attracted him? "The water," of course!

Above: The rather large portrait of the nude hanging over Fred's bed was hauled back from a thrift store on the West Dixie Highway. It was a bargain at $10.
Right: A city conversation captured in oil by Fred Bernstein's father. The lamp is from Target, the candle apple from Pottery Barn, and the stack of books from various secondhand bookstores.

The most personal item in Fred's one-room universe is the painting that leans on the bedside table to the left of his bed. The sign—BERNSTEIN'S GYMNASIUM—seen on one of the buildings in the painting's upper right corner is a clue to the artist's identity. It all fits when Fred reveals that his father, a self-taught painter, was a phys. ed. trainer and high school football coach in Pittsburgh. Painted in the Sixties, the picture captures another era, probably in the Thirties or Forties. Fred had wanted the painting for years, and on one of his visits home, his father gave it to him. It is a poignant reminder that no matter how committed we are to shedding our possessions and reinventing our lives, it is hard to let go of the home truths we grew up with.

Fred doesn't need to create a special work space for himself. When he walks into his little oasis, work is over. Still, a table is vital for writing letters and checks and possibly for setting down a plate for dinner. This one was found years ago at a Salvation Army store in New York City. It looks almost like a trestle drafting table, a resemblance that is enhanced by the old wooden paint box left by a visiting artist friend. The bulbous carved wooden sculpture is actually a Balinese lamp made from a coconut. The painting of a torso was bought in the same shop on the West Dixie Highway as the nude, opposite, for $6. The two chairs were discovered in a pile in a junk shop in Miami Beach. When Fred saw them he knew they were valuable. "I checked out the stamp on the bottom and called a savvy friend of mine who had invested in eight of the same chairs and a table for $6,000. She verified my instincts. I got them for $25 apiece!" He thinks they were designed by Hans Vegnen, a renowned modernist furniture designer. Maybe the truth will come out on an episode of *Antiques Roadshow*.

Above: The table, the torso, the coconut carved lamp, the wooden paint box, the pair of honey veneered chairs, all play by Fred's rules of thrift and calm. His investment: $138.50. Junker's worth: priceless!

NESTING

Anita Calero's quiet refuge for taking pictures was once a boisterous printing factory.

Anita Calero likes everything in its place. When she was a child growing up in South America, her orderliness made her brother and sister a little crazy. With one of those labeling machines, she created signs for each of her bureau drawers—T-shirts, sweaters, shorts—to assure that nothing would get mixed up. She admits her organized life even drives her a little crazy, but she could live no other way. Her loft floating high over New York City in a prewar building was originally a printing factory. In the Eighties, architects and artists looking for well-lit, open space started moving in. When she applied for an apartment three years ago, the building had been entirely converted to a working residence for artists. Having devoted the previous five years to taking pictures of people and carefully arranged still lifes, she qualified. Her loft's main space is a large square room flooded with light. If you didn't know Anita, you might wonder if she had just moved in or even question whether she really lived here. The room is austere, almost gallerylike. What you would never suspect, standing in this clean oasis and knowing the owner's fastidiousness, is that Anita Calero is a ravenous collector! Her secret lies in selectivity and her disciplined strategies for display and storage. On the wall to the north end of her loft is an elegant light-wood cabinet with a little blackboard displayed starkly above it and a cone-shaped bright orange lampshade above them both. Carefully slide open the doors of the cabinet (opposite) and gasp at what is revealed inside—100 boxed collections of Anita's earthly delights.

The cabinet, circa 1946, by Jean Prouvé that stores her junkier collectibles is in a class by itself. The blackboard reminded her of the art of Mark Rothko.

Left: Inside the French modernist cabinet, Anita hides away not only her collections of storage containers, but also her stereo and TV—"I hate to see them!"
Preceding pages: It was her mother, Cecilia (note her personalized matches in the grouping), who started Anita's love affair with matches. She started to pick them up wherever she traveled. The El Diablo box was a classic in Colombia; the Three Stars is Belgian. The straw box, another childhood memento, once stored coasters, which was probably a better idea than its present contents—matches.

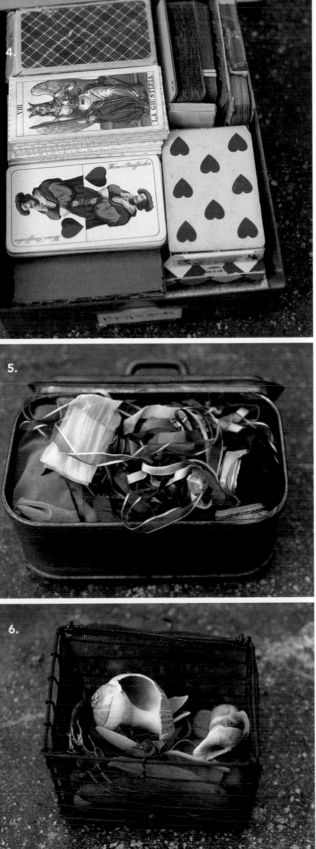

These pages, from left: **1.** The large white metal hospital box meant to store disinfected medical instruments was picked out among the clutter of a sidewalk sale table, on Canal Street in New York City, for $20. Inside you will find more little boxes storing diminutive things like buttons, corks, and pieces of wax. The photograph is a portrait of Anita's guru. "I like her tranquillity in that space," Anita remarks. **2.** Not only does Anita collect the things stored in the boxes—old and new postcards, metal and wooden forms, measuring devices, playing cards, cigarettes, matches, fans, papers, and pins—but she collects the boxes and assorted containers themselves. And she collects the myriad labels that identify them. She has found the labels in Paris, London, New York, and a special little shop in San Francisco called Bell'occhio. **3.** The stack of metal boxes designed to store syringes and medical supplies was gathered at Arista Medical Supply on Lexington Avenue at 26th Street, New York City. Made in Germany, they cost from $20 to $40 each, depending on the size. Today they store the romantic supplies of Anita's imagination—postcards, papers, and feathers, of course! **4.** Her fascination with cards started at her mother's side as she played bridge. Later, as a photographer, Anita was inspired by that famous photograph taken by Irving Penn in 1947, *After Dinner Games.* "I don't know how to play cards," she confesses, "but I love to add them to my pictures." **5.** The fanciful ribbons collected and recycled from presents are in contrast to the strict lines of the galvanzied French bread box she haggled for at a Paris flea market for $10. **6.** This wire-and-screen box was described to her as a Chinese cricket box. (She's not sure about the Chinese part.) In it are things swept up by the sea—pieces of shells, a blue balloon, driftwood twigs, smooth stones.

Above: Anita Calero organizes her files in recycled wooden wine crates along a shelf supported by an old iron radiator. Everything seems placed not only for efficiency, but for a certain aesthetic alignment.

The perfect application of her organizing principles is demonstrated in Anita's studio office. It is a long narrow space dominated by one large window and a whitewashed brick wall. Against the brick wall, seen above, and built on top of the old iron radiator camouflaged in white, is a narrow wooden shelf just wide enough to hold an antique portrait and a pair of wine-crate file boxes. To the right of the radiator is a tall tower of drawers labeled by content in much the way she kept her wardrobe sorted as a child.

Opposite: The pastel portrait of a young man from the turn of the century was spotted by Anita some years back through the window of a charmingly cluttered shop on the Upper East Side of Manhattan. The shopkeeper, Vito Giallo, told Anita that a very old man had brought it in one day and revealed that he was the boy in the pastel likeness. For many years Giallo had enjoyed the portrait hanging above his bed, but of late he thought it had induced nightmares. Anita loved the likeness, particularly his style of dress, and she loved the romance the young man brought to her spartan work area. Her investment in him was $500.

Left: The skinny tower of storage drawers, picked up by Anita at Ikea, was transformed by adding little polished steel grommets designed for portfolios for use as drawer pulls. Each drawer is assigned a duty by self-created labels.

Below: The five storage squares piled on top of each other like children's blocks were secured at Paula Rubenstein's antique store in New York City. On the top rests a horn bowl. Tucked inside are jars of grommets, stamps and coins from all her trips, rolls of tape, bottles of ink, and all her eyeglass cases.

MRC on the prowl at Lakewood.

Lakewood is huge! Ten acres, 1,200 dealers and six huge warehouses filled to the brim!

Most of the Atalanta junk shops are installed in strip malls. It's what's inside that counts!

Body shop art and a message.

Buttons tell the message. I picked up two from NY for a $1 each! They're the personal billboard.

A roundup of Big City dogs, sounds, and snaps.

Doesn't matter the size, every flea market has something to offer. I loved the palm tree mural.

A smorgasbord of dribs and drabs: every-

Atlanta under glass, $35.

Learn while you eat! A tray serving up the USA for $20, from a dealer's table at Lakewood.

At My Favorite Place, a dozen work gloves, $2,

Don't let the modern skyline fool you. Atlanta still has a lot of that old Southern charm.

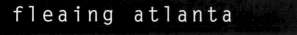

fleaing atlanta

If you fly to Atlanta the second weekend of the month, go directly to the Lakewood flea market

Dealers line up first!

Prize find! A '50s garage and line-up of vehicles, $40 at the Lakewood Market. Big City Junk supreme!

The action at Lakewood Antiques Market, held the second weekend of the month, starts on Thursday, Dealer's Day, through Sunday.

Advertising collectibles galore!

thing from life jackets to bedpans.

A bird's-eye view of the Lakewood Flea Market — ten acres of trash and treasure.

The kind of sign that gets my heart a-pounding.

Pick a chair, any chair at the Lakewood Antiques Market. $15 looks like the lucky number...I tried $10 and scored.

If you're going to pick up any Coca-Cola collectibles, count on Atlanta, the world headquarters.

Ben Apfelbaum, my Atlanta junking buddy!

Junking in Atlanta is not complete without some Smokey's Bar-B-Q.

I succumb to junk... food!

and junk, junk, junk! It will be hard to tear yourself away, but break for a junk jaunt into Atlanta proper. It's got junk with a southern accent, y'all!

207

ORIENT EXPRESS

I have wandered happily through Chinatown in San Francisco and in New York, Little Havana in Miami, and Little Italy in New York. Each community offers a jolt of a different spirit, a different culture tucked in a pocket of a big American city, each celebrating its own varied traditions, rituals, costumes, foods, and, of course, types of junk! Of all of them, Chinatown in lower Manhattan is probably the best known in general, and for me personally, the most familiar. Though I have made many trips there over the last twenty-five years, I now have a son living right in the thick of it, which magnifies my motivation to visit the neighborhood, giving me an almost insider's view. Chinatown, however, is certainly not the resource for all of the Asian treasures presented over the next several pages. Coming from a number of different countries, they can be hunted down in all major cities, in souvenir shops, in flea markets, on sidewalks, at tag sales, and, lest we forget, on the ubiquitous World Wide Web! The little chorus line, seen above, welcoming you into this Oriental folly was assembled from all over the junker's globe. The mysterious elder bedecked in the jeweled colors of an opulent robe, a $10 lamp seen at left, was literally picked up off the street in downtown Manhattan. Wandering off the beaten path to discover something different—call it exotic—is the path that we junkers have chosen. You need no map, unless you find one like I did on page 214. Just follow your instincts and head East!

Above: A welcoming committee of Chinese and Japanese figurines, mostly of souvenir quality, are lined up along the edge of a Chinatown pennant from Los Angeles. In the background is the decorated cover from a Chinese checkers game box. Nothing in the picture cost more than $5.
Left: Framed against the doorway of a graffitied doorway in New York's SoHo, a chipped chalkware lamp of a Chinese elder costumed in richly colored robes. The sidewalk tale of how I found him will unfold as you turn the page.

Sidewalk Story

It was a Sunday in June when my son Carter and I were on the prowl for city booty. We were casing the streets not too far from the SoHo flea market on lower Broadway when we came upon the little sidewalk street sale, seen above. I spotted the lamp right away and then introduced myself to Eddie, the seller, and asked him, "How much?" He asked me what I would like to invest, and I responded, "Five dollars." My son rolled his eyes at me, and before Eddie could respond, I doubled my offer to $10. Eddie was beaming. Carter seemed satisfied, and I got my prize and walked off into the sunset, looking forward to the next junker's showdown.

Above: A Japanese girl in bright red-and-green pajamas plays the samisen in the snow. The lamp was $10 at the Grand Bazaar, West 26th Street, New York City. **Left:** At her new home in our apartment in New York City, the little chipped musician is shaded by one of those green metal shades picked up at another city flea market (seen on page 65) for $2.50.

The little musician, at left, one of the three Asian lamps that light our New York City life, was rescued from a February snowstorm at the Grand Bazaar flea market on West 26th Street. I ventured out that freezing Sunday morning, wondering if any brave souls would be around, and was rewarded with lamp-in-snow, seen above. One of my favorite dealers, a hearty soul, reduced the price to $10 (snow sale!). When I got the lamp home and dried it off, I cautiously plugged it in—it worked! But don't trust old wiring. If you took those 4-H club sessions on rewiring a lamp, you can probably do it yourself. If, like me, you missed them, then find a hardware store or electrician to do the job. Don't leave anything to chance.

In my last book, *Kitchen Junk*, I told the story of a good friend, Bobby Ball, who having brought home a new/old green graniteware roasting pan, proceeded to redo his whole kitchen. Bobby's experience exemplifies the fun of finding something and then creating a home for it. This was exactly the situation when I brought home the little Chinese figurine seen at left. When I got her home I instinctively placed her near someone that I imagined was next of kin—the tall Chinese warrior guarding the table on the opposite page. Before she joined him, he was the lone, slightly out-of-place foreigner living in a landscape of Early American artifacts. After she arrived, I was awarded the tall Asian gentleman lamp as a farewell gift from our no-longer-store in Virginia—American Junk. Now with this dominant threesome in residence, everything else is seen in a more exotic light.

Left: I could hardly contain myself after I purchased this lovely Chinese princess offering a handful of flowers. On the way home from the Green Flea on 67th Street and York Avenue, New York City, where I purchased her for $5, I stopped to take her picture on the sidewalk in front of a black iron fence that could have been the gates to her palace.
Opposite: On my little warped cricket table, once the domain of an all-American harvest of fish, books, a chessboard, and marble grapes, three new out-of-towners have set up a more eclectic dynamic. The floral painting behind them cost $1 at a tag sale in the country. The headless woman above them was a prop I was able to snag at an advertising shoot.

213

Halfway through the novel *Memoirs of a Geisha*, I spotted the elegant doll in the mustard-colored robe, seen on the bench at right, and opposite. She was easy to pick out amid the clutter of a dusty barn sale in upstate New York. Her ransom price was $45. Within a month I had paired her with her friend, seen also at right, found in a far more compatible environment, the SoHo flea market, seen opposite page, lower right. The pièce de résistance was the huge school map of China found nested in a box at a flea market not far from that dusty barn in upstate New York. Probably damaged by so many foldings, it had been taken in hand by some prudent conservator who adhered all the pieces to a cloth background. Measuring 5 by 6½ feet, it papered most of the wall I hung it on in Carter's old bedroom space. I tacked red fabric under it and wall-to-walled the floor with an old India print bedspread. The gilt-embellished bench (not Chinese, but the feeling seemed right), was a gift from Howard's mother. The framed print of the kimonoed young woman has hung on our bedroom wall for fifteen years. The pillow stack gives the feeling of a teahouse. The sage-looking elder to the far left, actually a wine bottle, rests on a throne of two sushi boards. My *King and I* fantasy soon came down and was replaced by more conventional guest room decor. The geishas, along with their elderly uncle, retreated to the quiet of our house in the country, but the map is still hanging in the city, in Howard's home office, where it is the backdrop to standing files, a TV set, and a fax machine.

Though maps don't really qualify as junk, they are something I always keep my eye out for. School maps in particular are at the top of my list. If you own *American Junk*, my first junk book, you'll see on page 17 a school map of the United States with a wooden roller at the base for pulling it down from the storage case attached to the wall over a blackboard. In a back issue of the English magazine *World of Interiors*, vintage maps wallpapered an entire bedroom. City map guides make perfect sense framed and hung in city residences. My personal favorite is a bird's-eye view of New York City, commissioned by American Airlines as a promotional piece for the New York's World Fair of 1964. It took 67,000 photographs of the city, 17,000 from the air, to compose this astonishing piece of cartography. It unfolds to 31 by 42 inches, and every minute detail was drawn by hand. Some day I'll frame it!

Clockwise from top left: The little octagonal box, decorated with a frieze of Chinese characters, is probably not very old. It was a gift from a pair of favorite dealers who run a wonderful little roadside junk shop, Collector's Corner, in Millerton, New York. You can buy them new at Pearl River Emporium, New York City. My pair of Chinese cotton slippers (think of them as summer espadrilles) were $5 at Pearl River. Geisha doll number 2 was brought home to play with geisha number 1, for $15 at the SoHo flea market. (Who says things are cheaper in the country?) The distinguished elder—actually a wine bottle—stands his ground on a pair of painted wooden sushi boards discovered at The Garage, New York City, for $35. The parasoled ladies, a pair of paint-by-number beauties framed in glass, were $20 on Lisa Durfee's eBay site.

Above: A china compote dish that tells a story in miniature paintings was $15 at the SoHo flea market, New York City.

Left: A needlepoint geisha performing on the samisen, $8 at the 26th Street flea market. Below, carefully applied to the inside top of an exquisite tin-lined tea storage box, a watercolor of elaborately dressed women at work in the fields. The box, about 15 by 12 by 12 inches deep, was $50 at The Garage, New York City.

Opposite: A pajama-clad ceramic princess with classic bangs, flower pom-poms, and a seductive red fan was whisked away at the Holy Cow Flea Market, Red Hook, New York, for $3. She reigns from an ersatz throne of broken shells and bits of colored paper that make up the lining to an exotic little jewelry box I salvaged from a flea market in upstate New York.

It's hard to say why we collect what we collect. For me, it was clearly Sayuri, the heroine of *Memoirs of a Geisha* by Arthur Golden, who got me hooked on my geisha theme. I found her in ceramic figurines, in needlepoint portraits, in watercolor papers, on colorful serving dishes, on lamps, in paint-by-number paintings, in wall plaques, in funky foam-core cutouts, and of course in my geisha dolls.

SANCTUARY

Bill's home turf, a quaint San Francisco alleyway, feels a lot like Paris, his home away from home.

The first time I walked into Aria, a little shop in the North Beach section of San Francisco, it was dusk and the interior of the store was lit with low, warm lights. It felt safe and secure, the way a church does in off-hours when nobody else is around. Bill Haskell, the shop's proprietor, is tall and soft-spoken, well suited to this sanctuary of, as he puts it, "antiques, art, junk, and funk." Years later, when he invited me to his apartment located in an alley just a walk away from Aria, I entered his personal sanctuary. He dates his collecting back to age fourteen when he discovered a pair of Victorian glass domes hidden in the basement of his home in a small town in New Jersey. They were filled with mementos from his English uncle's grandmother. There was a piece of stone fruit and a bird of some kind, preserved by a taxidermist, and other strange souvenirs. Bill took them to add a little mystery to his room until they were discovered and removed: "not suitable decor," he presumes, "for a young boy's room!" Nonetheless, the thought of the domes stuck with him and he began to search out his own mementos in antique stores, buying little things when he could. After school in Michigan, and ten years in Chicago renovating loft buildings and selling finds to dealers there and in Madison, Wisconsin, he eventually landed in San Francisco. Starting in 1988 he became a regular at the legendary Marin County flea market, and when it closed down in 1995, he opened Aria. He wanted to give his shop a short name, one that was old and somehow related to the Italian neighborhood. When Bill explained those criteria to a good friend, the friend thought for a moment and said, "You mean something like 'Aria'?" And that was that! In Italian, *aria* actually means "a breath of fresh air," which is what you feel when you walk through the door.

Aria's storefront windows reflect the distinctive row houses of San Francisco's North Beach.

Left: A souvenir chalk plaque, probably commemorating the opening of the Oakland Bay Bridge in the mid-Thirties. Bill picked it up at the Berkeley flea market for about $20. Here it's pictured a little larger than life, leaning against a piece of tin-pierced poetry.

Above: The only windows face the alley and are 13 feet high. Sunlight pours through them, not in the least inhibited by the cheesecloth curtains and long twists of charcoal-colored gauzy silk.

Bill's alley home is attained by a climb up steep wooden stairs that creak out their age and authenticity as you step from one to the next. It's the kind of place he always envisioned living in—"a dark urban joint," as he puts it. "I love the trash blowing down the alley." He's lived there since 1997, when he saw a sign being placed in a storefront window —LIVE IN NORTH BEACH. He had just lost a large old flat he had sublet in Russian Hill, and was wondering what he would do. He went right in and leased it immediately.

Left: The coffee table was made from an English steel box that stored Parliamentarian wigs. Bill committed $400 to it during his decade in Chicago, where he also had the steel base made. A theme of body parts is played out on top of it in the arm of a crucified Christ, $15, the head of a Mexican santo, $75, and a midcentury wooden drawing model, $30, all found at flea markets in Paris. The small porcelain bowl was "a major steal," reports Bill, for $5. The old hotel silver pitcher, $35, found at a flea market, passed some time at Aria before Bill brought it home as a vase for spring flowers. On top of the old ledger rests a book with an appropriate San Francisco title—*Beat Culture.*

Opposite, right: The photograph of the Eiffel Tower, a centerpiece of Bill's homes as long as he's had it, was from a collection from the Thirties. The cast-iron statue of the lady (one of his favorites) was found at a Wisconsin garage sale for $18. He collects jointed lamps of painted steel whenever he sees them, for $20 and up, and has them restored with vintage twisted cords. Beyond the knobbly sterling candlesticks from the Twenties are a pair of 200-year-old lamps fueled by yak butter, picked up in Nepal for $40. On the wall above them is a little calcitrated bronze pocket-watch case. The metal floral tray behind was found at a San Francisco estate sale for $75. The hammered copper bowls in front were retrieved from the Upper Peninsula of Michigan—the site of many old copper mines.

Above: The trade union poster of two French carpenters dates to the Twenties. Bill paid $100 for it at a Paris flea market.
Right: Bill, who once had an old cabin in the woods of northern Wisconsin, wanted his apartment to feel like being in those forests. He calls the color of his walls forest green, though it's closer to avocado. When the sun shines through his windows, it mutes the color like sun through the trees. He got the rare Mission bench for $1,000 only because he made sure he was at the flea market where it was to be sold at five in the morning. It sat for decades outside of an office in an old church in Oakdale that was demolished three years ago. Wrapped around the seat cushion is a vintage Mideastern textile. The little weaving hanging over the back is a Mexican tourist serape from the Thirties that he bought locally for $20. The handhewn walnut cross, found in a Paris flea market for $25, is at least two hundred years old. The nickel-plated clinical lamp was $40 at a Porte de Montruil flea market. On the wall above it is a historical photograph from an old lodge in northern Wisconsin. The beautiful scene of the natural world of the Sierra hanging above it was painted on a very unnatural piece of asbestos. Bill landed on it at a flea market in the Bay Area for $40. Keeping the rustic theme going, Bill tacked up an old iron wheel from a toy tractor above it.

"Where's the food and the pots and pans?" I shyly asked Bill as I surveyed the most romantic kitchen nook I had ever gazed upon. He explained he eats out a lot, but there are shelves curtained off to the right of the table where essentials like a toaster may be found. To the left of his quasi kitchen counter, you can detect the corner of a worthy stainless steel sink, but a stove has yet to be installed. Perhaps there is a hot plate hidden in the larder? Bill would rather fill his shopping cart with alabaster fruit from the flea market than with the kind that ripens and has to be replaced. He stores Bakelite, ivory, and bone dice in apothecary jars meant for storing spices and such. The closest thing to a chef in this kitchen is probably the bearded garden gnome seen on top of Bill's treasured silver-colored shelf that holds mostly non-kitchen items, a treasure bought from a bunch of barefoot kids at a barn in Wisconsin.

Left: The concrete garden gnome/ kitchen chef has been part of Bill's life for at least ten years; he was purchased for $75. The chalkware fruit bowl was picked up at a flea market at about the same time. Sprinkled throughout the apartment are old glass medicinal domes and fishing flats, wooden spheres and alabaster fruit. The steel dividers splayed open on the bottom shelf are an unusual size, which is why they cost about $50. The silver Deco percolator and turn-of-the-century shaving mirror aid morning wake-up rituals.

223

Above: The old brass Mission bed (painted white) was discovered at an estate sale in an old San Francisco house.

Right: The California light box came from a bikers' bar in Boise, Idaho. Bill got it from an antiques picker for $100. The Enro shirt man, an advertising piece from the Fifties, was snagged early one morning at the Alemany flea market (see page 88, for a tour) for $75. The numbered and drawered cabinet stores more dice, marbles, and business cards. After losing his pet springer spaniel of sixteen years, Bill is keeping the cast-iron Boston terrier doorstop, $100, until he decides to go for the real thing.

Bill's bedroom is out of range of natural light, so the room's main supply of illumination radiates from a Westinghouse countertop display fixture, seen above on the table to the right of his bed. He secured it for $150 from Figoni's, a landmark neighborhood hardware store, during its closeout sale. The award for the longest-lasting light source goes to the flicker bulb encased inside the vaseline glass teardrop-shaped case set in a cast-iron escutcheon base attached to the wall to the left of the State of California. For four years Bill has never turned it off, and it's still going. The lamp was a $50 flea market find. The flicker bulb, available today, was $4.

224

Above: Hopefully, the drawers of this old green Mission-style dresser don't stick. If they do, all of Bill's hard work in designing his dresser-top tableau will be ruined with one good pull. The sturdy Red Cross bank that made his heart flutter when he spotted it at the Marin County flea market years ago, for $50, would undoubtedly survive. You could probably count on the twig lamp with the orange parchment shade to make it as well. The old loving cup/vase, a great buy for $20 at the Alemany flea, could withstand even a mild tremor. But the heavy rubber farm animals grazing across the top of the dresser would probably lose their footing, as would the flat wooden jointed mannequin to the left of the cross. The doomed list might include the alabaster light to the far right, the tall wallpaper roller filled with arrows next to it, and the glass dome reminiscent of the pair Bill uncovered in his childhood basement. Safe on the wall to the left is the painting of *Fluffy Flowers*, picked up on a road trip through California. The birch branch below it was recovered after a tornado. The tiny wooden grate balanced above it is a primitive screen for a little window. The ladder to the far right leaning against the wall leads to a tiny loft.

ATLANTA

Lakewood Antiques Market
I-75 to Exit 88, East on 166 to
The Lakewood Fairgrounds **(404) 622-4488**
The second weekend of every month
Friday & Saturday, 9:00 a.m.–6:00 p.m.
Sunday, 10:00 a.m.–5:00 p.m.

My Favorite Place
5596 Peachtree Industrial Boulevard
Chamblee, GA 30341   **(770) 452-8397**
Open daily, 10:00 a.m.–5:30 p.m.

Scavenger Hunt
3438 Clairmont Road
Atlanta, GA 30319   **(404) 634-4948**
Open daily, 10:00 a.m.–6:00 p.m.

Scott Antiques Market
Atlanta Exposition Center
I-285 to Exit 55 (Jonesboro Rd.) **(740) 569-4112**
The second weekend of every month
Friday & Saturday, 9:00 a.m.–6:00 p.m.
Sunday, 10:00 a.m.–4:00 p.m.

BOSTON

Bobby From Boston
19 Thayer Street
Boston, MA 02118   **(617) 423-9299**
Monday–Saturday, 12:00 p.m.–6:00 p.m.
(An appointment is preferable.)

Buckaroo's Mercantile
858 Massachusetts Avenue
Cambridge, MA 02139   **(617) 864-3637**
Monday–Friday, 1:00 p.m.–9:00 p.m.
Saturday, 11:00 a.m.–10:00 p.m.
Sunday, 11:00 a.m.–5:00 p.m.

Old, but new!

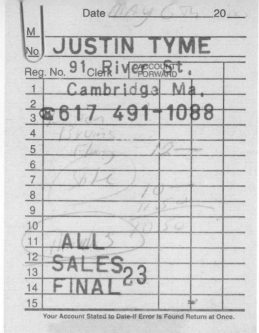

Date MAY 6, 20
M No.
JUSTIN TYME
Reg. No. 91 River St.
Cambridge, Ma.
☎ 617 491-1088
ALL SALES FINAL

Your Account Stated to Date-If Error Is Found Return at Once.

Cambridge Antique Market
201 Msgr. O'Brien Highway
Cambridge, MA 02141   **(617) 868-9655**
Tuesday–Sunday, 11:00 a.m–6:00 p.m.

The Collector
63 Harvard Avenue
Allston, MA 02134   **(617) 787-5952**
Open daily, 11:00 a.m.–6:00 p.m.

Hadassah Bargain Spot
1123 Commonwealth Avenue
Boston, MA 02215   **(617) 254-8300**
Sunday–Thursday, 10:00 a.m.–5:30 p.m.
Friday, 10:00 a.m.–2:00 p.m.

Justin Tyme Emporium
91 River Street
Cambridge, MA 02139   **(617) 491-1088**
Wednesday–Friday, 1:00 p.m.–6:00 p.m.
Saturday, 11:00 a.m.–6:00 p.m.
Sunday, 1:00 p.m.–4:00 p.m.

Lush Life Antiques
17 Harvard Avenue
Allston, MA 02134   **(617) 787-7878**
Monday–Saturday, 11:00 a.m.–6:00 p.m.
Sunday, 12:00 p.m.–6:00 p.m.

Mr. and Mrs. Bartley's Burger Cottage
(Grab a bite in an "academic environment"!)
1246 Massachusetts Avenue
Cambridge, MA 02139   **(617) 354-6559**
Closed Sunday

The Museum of Bad Art
580 High Street
Dedham Community Theater (in the basement)
Route 1/Dedham Center (about 8 miles south
of downtown Boston)   **(617) 325-8224**
Monday–Friday, 6:30 p.m.–10:00 p.m.
Saturday & Sunday, 1:00 p.m.–10:00 p.m.
Free Admission (and worth every penny of it!)

Rentparty
180 River Street
Cambridge, MA 02139   **(617) 661-6964**
Incredible place, hit or miss hours!
Just hope you get lucky!

Suzette Sundae's
167 Brighton Avenue
Allston, MA 02134   **(617) 254-4678**
Wednesday–Saturday, 11:00 a.m.–6:00 p.m.
Sunday, 12:00 p.m.–5:00 p.m.

CHICAGO

Ark Thrift
3345 North Lincoln Avenue
Chicago, IL 60657   **(773) 929-0200**
Monday & Thursday, 10:30 a.m.–7:00 p.m.
Tuesday & Wednesday, 10:30 a.m.–6:00 p.m.
Sunday, 11:00 a.m.–5:00 p.m.

Two junk divas pose for a polaroid!

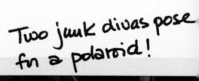

Suzette Sundae's
167 brighton ave.
allston, ma 02134
617.254.4678

Bongo Room
(A cool enviroment for respite and refueling)
1470 North Milwaukee Avenue
Chicago, IL 60622 **(773) 489-0690**
Monday–Friday, 8:00 a.m.–2:30 p.m.
Saturday & Sunday, 9:30 a.m.–2:30 p.m.

Broadway Antique Market
6130 North Broadway
Chicago, IL 60660 **(773) 743-5444**
Monday–Saturday, 11:00 a.m.–7:00 p.m.
Sunday, 12:00 p.m.–6:00 p.m.

Brooke James Ltd.
1460 North Milwaukee Avenue
Chicago, IL 60622 **(773) 252-4620**
Wednesday–Saturday, 11:00 a.m.–6:00 p.m.
Sunday, 11:00 a.m.–5:00 p.m.

Chicago Antique Center, LTD.
3045 North Lincoln Avenue
Chicago, IL 60657 **(773) 929-0200**
Open daily, 11:00 a.m.–6:00 p.m.

Danger City
2129 West Belmont Avenue
Chicago, IL 60618 **(773) 871-1420**
Open daily, 11:00 a.m.–6:00 p.m.

Lincoln Avenue Antique Coop
3851 North Lincoln Avenue
Chicago, IL 60613 **(773) 935-6600**
Tuesday–Saturday, 12:00 p.m.–6:00 p.m.

The ticket to junking is always free!

ADMIT ONE
308865 308865
GOOD DATE OF SALE ONLY
Weldon, Williams & Lick

YOUR RECEIPT

THANK YOU

SALVATION ARMY·ARC
CHICAGO
312-438-4360

10:30AM   JAN 19/00
01-0001 003   CASH 1
#01908   TAWAN

WM CLOTHING 1$7.00
MDSE $7.00
TAX1 $0.61

*TTL $7.61
CASH $20.00
CHANGE $12.39

THANKS FOR SHOPPING
AT THE SALVATION ARMY
ALL ITEMS SOLD AS IS

Pursuing the Past Mall
2229 West Belmont Avenue
Chicago, IL 60618 **(773) 871-3915**
Open daily, 11:00 a.m.–6:00 p.m.

Red Eye
3050 North Lincoln Avenue
Chicago, IL 60657 **(773) 975-2020**
Open daily, 12:00 p.m.–6:00 p.m.

Robin Richman
(A fashion boutique with extraordinary vintage fixtures and décor)
2108 North Damen Avenue
Chicago, IL 60647 **(773) 278-6150**
Tuesday–Saturday, 11:00 a.m.–6:00 p.m.
Sunday, 12:00 p.m.–5:00 p.m.

The Salvation Army Thrift Store
509 North Union Avenue
Chicago, IL 60610 **(312) 438-4360**
Open daily, 10:00 a.m.–6:00 p.m.

Strange
3448 North Clark Street
Chicago, IL 60657 **(773) 327-8090**
Monday–Saturday, 11:30 a.m.–6:45 p.m.
Sunday, 12:00 p.m.–5:30 p.m.

Vintage Deluxe
2127 West Belmont Avenue
Chicago, IL 60618 **(773) 529-7008**
Wednesday–Monday, 12:00 p.m.–6:00 p.m.

Uncle Fun (Childhood junk; old and new)
1338 West Belmont Avenue
Chicago, IL 60657 **(773) 477-8223**
Wednesday–Friday, 12:00 p.m.–7:00 p.m.
Saturday, 11:00 a.m.–7:00 p.m.
Sunday, 12:00 p.m.–5:00 p.m.

DALLAS

Affordable Antiques Plus
1201 North Industrial Boulevard
Dallas, TX 75207 **(214) 741-2121**
Wednesday–Saturday, 10:00 a.m.–5:00 p.m.
Sunday, 12:00 p.m.–5:00 p.m.

Bettyann & Jimbo's Antique Marketplace
4402 West Lovers Lane
Dallas, TX 75209
(214) 350-5755
Monday–Saturday,
10:00 a.m.–6:00 p.m.
Sunday,
12:00 p.m.–5:00 p.m.

Check out their backyard fun!

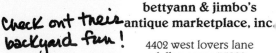

Cool Junk
2924 Main Street
Dallas, TX 75226 **(214) 741-2002**
Wednesday–Sunday, 12:00 p.m.–6:00 p.m.

Country Garden Antiques
147 Parkhouse Street
Dallas, TX 75207 **(214) 741-9331**
Monday–Saturday, 11:00 a.m.–5:00 p.m.
Sunday by appointment

HMI Architectural Salvage
200 Corinth Street
Dallas, TX 75207 **(214) 422-1888**
Wednesday–Saturday, 9:00 a.m.–5:00 p.m.

Forestwood Antique Mall
5333 Forest Lane
Dallas, TX 75244 **(927) 661-0001**
Monday–Saturday, 10:00 a.m.–7:00 p.m.

The Homestead
(If you plan to wander out of Dallas!)
223 East Main Street
Fredericksburg, TX 78624 **(830) 997-5551**
Monday–Saturday,
10:30 a.m.–5:30 p.m.
Sunday,
1:00 p.m.–5:00 p.m.

legacy trading co

james turner

2800 routh st #150

dallas, texas 75201

214.953.2222 fax 214.220.9051

Liberty & Son's
1506 Market Center Boulevard
Dallas, TX 75207 **(214) 748-3329**
Monday–Saurday, 10:00 a.m.–4:00 p.m.

Lower Greenville Antique Mall
2010 Greenville Avenue
Dallas, TX 75206 **(214) 824-4136**
Monday–Saturday, 10:00 a.m.–5:30 p.m.
Sunday, 12:00 p.m.–5:30 p.m.

Love Field Antique Mall
6500 Cedar Springs
Dallas, TX 75235 **(214) 357-6500**
Monday–Saturday, 10:00 a.m.–7:00 p.m.
Sunday, 12:00 p.m.–7:00 p.m.

Lula B's Antique Mall
2002 Greenville Avenue
Dallas, TX 72206 **(214) 824-2185**
Monday–Saturday, 11:00 a.m.–7:00 p.m.
Sunday, 12:00 p.m.–7:00 p.m.

Mary Cates and Co.
2700-2706 Boll Street
Dallas, TX 75204 **(214) 871-7953**
Monday–Saturday, 10:00 a.m.–5:00 p.m.

Park Cities Antique Mall
4908 West Lovers Lane
Dallas, TX 75225 **(214) 350-5983**
Monday–Saturday, 10:00 a.m.–6:00 p.m.
Sunday, 12:00 p.m.–6:00 p.m.

Room Service
4354 Lovers Lane
Dallas, TX 75225 **(214) 369-7666**
Monday–Friday, 10:00 a.m.–5:30 p.m.
Saturday, 10:00 a.m.–5:00 p.m.

Sticks and Stones Garden Market
5016 Miller Avenue
Dallas, TX 75206 **(214) 824-7277**
Monday, 12:00 p.m.–6:00 p.m.
Tuesday–Saturday, 10:00 a.m.–6:00 p.m.
Sunday, 12:00 p.m.–5:00 p.m.

Legacy Trading Co.
2800 Routh Street
#150
Dallas, TX 75201
(214) 953-2222
Monday–Thursday,
11:00 a.m.–7:00 p.m.
Friday & Saturday,
11:00 a.m.–8:00 p.m.
Sunday,
12:00 p.m.–5:00 p.m.

Uncommon Market
2701 Fairmount Street
Dallas, TX 75201 **(214) 871-2775**
Monday–Saturday, 10:00 a.m.–5:30 p.m.

Decorative — Antiques

UNCOMMON MARKET

2701 FAIRMOUNT • DALLAS, TEXAS 75201 • 214 871-2775
Ward Mayborn *Incorporated 1973* **Don Mayborn**

Break for a Texas junkburger!

Uncommon Objects
1512 South Congress Avenue
Austin, TX 78704 **(512) 442-4000**
Sunday–Thursday, 11:00 a.m.–6:00 p.m.
Friday & Saturday, 11:00 a.m.–7:00 p.m.

Webb Gallery
209–211 West Franklin Street
Waxahachie, TX 75165 **(972) 938-8085**
Saturday & Sunday, 1:00 p.m.–5:00 p.m.

WHITE ELEPHANT
Antiques & Gifts
1026 N. Industrial Blvd.
(214) 871-7966
Hours: 10-5, Mon.-Sat.

White Elephant Antiques Warehouse
1026 North Industrial Boulevard
Dallas, TX 75207 **(214) 871-7966**
Monday–Saturday, 10:00 a.m.–5:00 p.m.
Sunday, 1:00 p.m.–5:00 p.m.

White Elephant Architectural & Garden Station
1130 North Industrial Boulevard
Dallas, TX 75207 **(214) 871-7966**
Monday–Saturday, 10:00 a.m.–5:00 p.m.
Sunday, 1:00 p.m.–5:00 p.m.

Wrecking Barn
1421 North Industrial Boulevard
Dallas, TX 75207   **(214) 747-2777**
Tuesday–Friday, 9:00 a.m.–5:00 p.m.
Saturday, 10:00 a.m.–3:00 p.m.

LOS ANGELES

A. N. Abell Auction Company
2613 Yates Avenue
Los Angeles, CA 90040   **(323) 724-8102**
Auctions every Thursday, 9 a.m.
Website: *Abell.com*

Bargain Bazaar Thrift Store
1435 15th Street
Santa Monica, CA 90404   **(310) 395-2338**
Tuesday, Thursday, Friday & Saturday, 11 a.m.–3 p.m.
(Go early Tuesday mornings to see the new stuff!)

Bountiful (Go just to be inspired!)
1335 Abbot Kinney Boulevard
Venice, CA 90291   **(310) 450-3620**
Monday–Saturday, 10:00 a.m.–5:00 p.m.
Sunday, 12:00 p.m.–5:00 p.m.

Claire Foundation Thrift Store
850 Pico Boulevard
Los Angeles, CA 90404   **(310) 314-6241**
Monday–Friday, 9:00 a.m.–5:00 p.m.
Saturday, 10:00 a.m.–4:00 p.m.

Community Thrift Store
427 North Fairfax Avenue
Los Angeles, CA 90036   **(323) 655-3110**

Shari Elf
(Has moved to Kansas City!)
You can see her work on her website, *Sharielf.com*

Haywire
5247 Melrose Avenue
Hollywood, CA 90038   **(323) 466-6676**
Monday–Saturday, 1:00 p.m.–6:00 p.m.
Sunday, 12:00 p.m.–5:00 p.m.

323
–
466
–
6676

Furniture & Accessories Of The 20TH Century
Moderne, Art Deco, 40's, 50's & 60's
5247 MELROSE AVE., HOLLYWOOD, CA 90038

Lagitana
7829 Melrose Avenue (right near the Melrose Trading Post)
Los Angeles, CA 90046   **(323) 653-1508**
Monday–Saturday, 12:00 p.m.–7:00 p.m.
Sunday, 10:00 a.m.–6:00 p.m.

Liz's Antique Hardware
453 South La Brea Avenue
Los Angeles, CA 90036   **(213) 939-4403**
Open daily, 10:00 a.m.–6:00 p.m.

Long Beach Outdoor Antiques and Collectibles Market
Veteran Memorial Stadium on Conant Street
   between Lakewood and Clark Boulevards
Long Beach, CA 90808   **(213) 655-5703**
Third Sunday of every month, 6:30 a.m.–3:00 p.m.
Admission: $4.50

The Melrose Trading Post
Fairfax High School
7850 Melrose Avenue   **(323) 651-5200**
Every Sunday. Admission: $2, students and seniors $1

Orange (Mostly restored)
245 South Robertson Boulevard
Beverly Hills, CA 90211   **(310) 652-5195**
Monday–Saturday, 10:00 a.m.–6:00 p.m.

ORANGe
furnishings + home design

Out of the Closet Thrift Store (One of 14!)
360 Fairfax Avenue
Los Angeles, CA 90036   **(323) 934-1956**
Monday–Saturday, 8:30 a.m.–7:00 p.m.
Sunday, 9:00 a.m.–6:00 p.m.

Pasadena City College Flea Market
1570 East Colorado Boulevard
Pasadena, CA 91106   **(626) 585-7906**
First Sunday of every month, 8:00 a.m.–3:00 p.m.
Admission: Free

Forget the freeway,
go Alleying in LA!
See page 129!

Rose Bowl Flea Market
1001 Rose Bowl Drive
Pasadena, CA 91103   **(213) 587-5100**
Second Sunday of every month, 9:00 a.m.–3:00 p.m.
Admission: $5.00

Scavenger's Paradise
5453 Satsuma Avenue
North Hollywood, CA 91604   **(323) 877-7945**
Monday–Saturday, 10:00 a.m.–4:30 p.m.
(or by appointment)

David Yarborough
1005 Mission Street
South Pasadena, CA 91030   (No Phone)
Open daily, 10:00 a.m.–5:00 p.m.

MIAMI

American Salvage
7001 Northwest 27th Street
Miami, FL 33142   **(305) 691-7001**
Monday–Friday, 8:00 a.m.–5:00 p.m.
Saturday, 8:00 a.m.–5:00 p.m.

Douglas Garden Thrift Shop
5713–37 Northwest 27th Avenue
Miami, FL 33142   **(305) 638-1900**
Monday—Saturday, 9:00 a.m.–5:15 p.m.
Sunday, 10:00 a.m.–5:00 p.m.

Faith Farm
1980 Northwest 9th Avenue
Fort Lauderdale, FL 33311 **(945) 763-7787**
Thursday–Monday, 9:00 a.m.–8:00 p.m.

Flamingo Plaza
901 East 10th Avenue
Hialeah, FL 33010 **(305) 888-8152**
Monday–Friday, 9:00 a.m.–6:00 p.m.

Fly Boutique
650 Lincoln Road
Miami Beach, FL 33139 **(305) 604-8508**
Open daily, 12:00 p.m.–10:00 p.m.

Jean Marie Deardorff · Fabian Giannnattasio

fly boutique
men & women

650 Lincoln Road Miami Beach Fl 33139
tel/fax 305 604-8508

Lincoln Road Mall
Lincoln Road (between Meridian and Washington)
Sundays

Patti Stoecker
Miami Beach, FL **(305) 531-5998**
www.poshvintage.com
Call for an appointment

Stone Age Antiques
3236 N. W. So. River Drive
Miami, FL 33142 **(305) 633-5114**
www.stoneage-antiques.com

Swap Shop
3291 West Sunrise Boulevard
Fort Lauderdale, FL 33311 **(954) 791-7927**
Monday–Friday, 6:00 a.m.–5:00 p.m.
Saturday & Sunday, 5:00 a.m.–6:00 p.m.

Vanity Novelty Garden
919 Fourth Street
Miami Beach, FL 33139 **(305) 534-6115**
By appointment only

Vintage Soul
1235 Alton Road
Miami Beach, FL 33139 **(305) 538-2644**
Monday–Saturday, 11:00 a.m.–7:00 p.m.
Sunday, 2:00 p.m.–6:00 p.m.

JUNK IN The City—
go No further!

World Resources
718 Lincoln Road
Miami Beach, FL 33139 **(305) 535-8987**
Monday–Friday, noon–11:00 p.m.
Saturday & Sunday, noon–12:30 a.m.

NEW YORK CITY

Anthropologie
375 West Broadway
New York, NY 10012 **(212) 343-7070**
Monday–Saturday, 11:00 a.m.–8:00 p.m.
Sunday, 11:00 a.m.–6:00 p.m.

The Annex
(Most New Yorkers call it "the 26th St. flea")
Sixth Avenue and West 26th Street
New York, NY **(212) 243-5343**
Saturday & Sunday, sunrise to sunset
Admission: $1

Atomic Passion
430 East Ninth Street
New York, NY 10009 **(212) 533-0718**
Open daily, 1:00 p.m.–9:00 p.m.

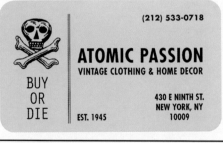

(212) 533-0718

ATOMIC PASSION
VINTAGE CLOTHING & HOME DECOR

BUY OR DIE

EST. 1945

430 E NINTH ST.
NEW YORK, NY
10009

Call Again Thrift Shop
1711 First Avenue
New York, NY 10128 **(212) 831-0845**
Monday–Saturday, 10:00 a.m.–4:30 p.m.

Cosmos
314 Wythe Avenue
Brooklyn, NY 11211 **(718) 302-4662**
Wednesday–Sunday, 12:00 p.m.–7:00 p.m.

Craft Caravan
63 Greene Street
New York, NY 10012 **(212) 431-6669**
Monday–Friday, 10:30 a.m.–6:30 p.m.
Saturday & Sunday, 11:30 a.m.–6:30 p.m.

David Davis Artist Materials & Services
17 Bleecker Street
New York, NY 10012 **(212) 260-9544**
Monday–Friday, 9:30 a.m.–6:00 p.m..
Saturday, 11:00 a.m.–6:00 p.m.

No admission to a
De La Vega exhibit!

De La Vega
1651 Lexington Avenue
New York, NY 10029 **(212) 876-8649**
Monday–Saturday, 11:00 a.m.–7:00 p.m.
Sunday, 11:00 a.m.–5:30 p.m.

Diner
(Go for brunch after a morning of junking)
85 Broadway
Brooklyn, NY 11211 **(718) 486-3077**
Opens at 11:00 a.m.

Dosa
107 Thompson Street
New York, NY 10012 **(212) 431-1733**
Monday–Saturday, 12:00 p.m.–7:00 p.m.
Sunday, 12:00 p.m.–6:00 p.m.

Dullsville
143 East 13th Street
New York, NY 10003 **(212) 505-2505**
Wednesday–Saturday, 12:00 p.m.–7:00 p.m.

15-smake   2 for 45
tin box-10   sign-12

Lisa Durfee
Go to her eBay site under durlink
Email her at *durflink@valstar.net*
Or find her most Sundays at
The Elephant Trunk Flea Market
Route 7
New Milford, CT 06776　　**(860) 355-1448**
Sundays only, 7:00 a.m.–3:00 p.m.

Empire Diner
(Close to the 26th Street flea!)
210 Tenth Avenue (at 22nd Street)
New York, NY 10011　　**(212) 243-2736**
Daily, 24 hours

Fishs Eddy
889 Broadway (at 19th Street)
New York, NY 10003　　**(212) 420-9020**
Monday–Saturday, 10:00 a.m.–8:00 p.m.
Sunday, 11:00 a.m.–7:00 p.m.

2176 Broadway (at 77th Street)
New York, NY 10024　　**(212) 873-8819**
Monday–Saturday, 10:00 a.m.–9:00 p.m.
Sunday, 11:00 a.m.–8:00 p.m.
www.fishseddy.com

G & S Designs—Warning!!! Junk Shop
324 Wythe Avenue
Brooklyn, NY 11211　　**(718) 388-8580**
Wednesday–Sunday, 12:00 p.m.–6:00 p.m.
Saturday, 12:00 p.m.–7:00 p.m.

The Garage
112 West 25th Street
New York, NY　　**(212) 647-0707**
Saturday & Sunday, sunrise to sunset

The Grand Bazaar Flea Market
West 25th Street (between Fifth & Sixth Avenues)
Saturday & Sunday, sunrise to sunset

Green Flea Markets
West 77th Street & Columbus Avenue
Sundays, 10:00 a.m–6:00 p.m.

East 67th Street & York Avenue
Saturdays, 6:00 a.m.–5:00 p.m.

Kitschen
380 Bleecker Street
New York, NY 10014　　**(212) 727-0430**
Open daily, except Tuesday, 2:00–8:00 p.m.

Northside Junk
578 Driggs Avenue
Williamsburg, Brooklyn 11211 **(718) 302-1045**
Monday, Thursday & Friday, 2:00 p.m.–7:00 p.m.
Saturday, 12:00 p.m.–8:00 p.m.
Sunday, 12:00 p.m.–6:00 p.m.

Olde Good Things
124 West 24th Street
New York, NY 10011　　**(212) 989-8401**
Friday–Sunday, 10:00 a.m.–Midnight
Monday–Thursday, 10:00 a.m.–8:00 p.m.

Pearl River
200 Grand Street
New York, NY 10013　　**(212) 966-1010**
Daily, 10:00 a.m.–7:30 p.m.

The Pop Shop
292 Lafayette Street
New York, NY 10012　　**(212) 219-2784**
Daily, 12:00 p.m.–7:00 p.m.
Sunday, 12:00 p.m.–6:00 p.m.

A Repeat Performance
156 First Avenue
New York, NY 10009
Monday–Saturday, 12:00 p.m.–8:00 p.m.
Sunday, 2:00 p.m.–8:00 p.m.

Paula Rubenstein
65 Prince Street
New York, NY 10012　　**(212) 966-8954**
Monday–Saturday, 12:00 p.m.–6:00 p.m.

Shi
233 Elizabeth Street
New York, NY 10012
Monday–Saturday, 12:00 p.m.–7:00 p.m.
Sunday, 12:00 p.m.–6:00 p.m.

Soho Antiques & Collectibles Flea Market
Broadway and Grand Street
New York, NY　　**(212) 682-2000**
Sundays, 9:00 a.m.–5:00 p.m.

Terra Firma
448 West 16th Street
New York, NY 10011　　**(212) 633-1862**
By appointment only

Thirty Bond
322 West 11th Street
New York, NY 10012　　**(212) 633-9889**
Daily, 2:00 p.m.–6:00 p.m., closed Wednesday

Two Jakes
320 Wythe Avenue
Brooklyn, New York 11211　**(718) 782-7780**
Wednesday–Sunday, 11:00 a.m.–7:00 p.m.

Ugly Luggage
214 Bedford Avenue
Brooklyn, New York 11211　**(718) 384-0724**
Monday–Friday, 1:00 p.m.–8:00 p.m.
Saturday & Sunday, 12:00 p.m.–6:00 p.m.

White Trash
304 East 5th Street
New York, NY 10003　　**(718) 782-7780**
Wednesday–Sunday, 11:00 a.m.–7:00 p.m.

If I can junk it here ...
I can junk it anywhere!

SAN FRANCISCO

Alemany Flea Market
101 South to 280 South,
Exit Alemany Boulevard   **(415) 647-2043**
Sundays, 7:00 a.m. until dusk

Aria
1522 Grant Avenue
San Francisco, CA 94133   **(415) 433-0219**
Open Daily, 12:00 p.m.–7:00 p.m.

Classic Consignment
867 Valencia Street
San Francisco, CA 94110   **(415) 550-0870**
Monday–Saturday, 11:30 a.m.–6:30 p.m.
Sunday, 12:00 p.m.–6:00 p.m.

Gypsy Honeymoon
3599 24th Street
San Francisco, CA 94110   **(415) 821-1713**
Wednesday, Saturday & Sunday,
11:00 a.m.–6:00 p.m.

Interieur Perdu
340 Bryant Street
San Francisco, CA 94107   **(415) 543-1616**
Monday–Saturday, 10:00 a.m.–5:00 p.m.
www.interieurperdu.com

Krim Krams
3611 18th Street
San Francisco, CA 94110   **(415) 626-1019**
Monday–Friday, 1:00 p.m.–6:00 p.m.
Saturday, 12:00 p.m.–6:30 p.m.
Sunday, 12:00 p.m.–6:00 p.m.

Light Opera
460 Post Street
San Francisco, CA 14102   **(415) 956-9866**
Monday–Saturday, 10:00 a.m.–5:30 p.m.
Sunday, 12:00 p.m.–5:00 p.m.

Mama's on Washington Square
(For Breakfast!)
1701 Stockton Street
San Francisco, CA 94133   **(415) 362-6421**
Tuesday–Sunday, 8:00 a.m.–3:00 p.m.)

Nest on Presidio
340 Presidio Avenue
San Francisco, CA 97115   **(510) 776-7289**
Monday–Saturday, 10:00 a.m.–6:00 p.m.

The Other Shop
112 Gough Street
San Francisco, CA 94102   **(415) 621-1590**
Monday–Saturday, 12:00 p.m.–6:00 p.m.
Sunday, 1:00 p.m.–6:00 p.m.

327 Divisadero Street
San Francisco, CA 94117   **(415) 621-5424**
Open daily, 12:00 p.m.–6:00 p.m.

Star
1415 Valencia Street
San Francisco, CA 94110   **(415) 282-9939**
Friday, Saturday & Sunday, 12:00 p.m.–6:00 p.m.

Tail of the Yak Trading
2632 Ashby Avenue
Berkeley, CA 94705   **(510) 841-9891**
Monday–Saturday, 11:00 a.m.–5:00 p.m.

Therapy
545 Valencia Street
San Francisco, CA 94110   **(415) 861-6213**
Monday–Friday, 12:00 p.m.–7:00 p.m.
Sunday, 11:00 a.m.–7:00 p.m.

Urban Ore
1333 Sixth Street
Berkeley, CA 94710   **(510) 235-0172**
Open daily, 8:30 a.m.–5:00 p.m.

Yard Art
2188 1/2 Sutter Street
San Francisco, CA 94115   **(415) 346-6002**
Friday & Saturday, 11:00 a.m.–5:00 p.m.
(or by appointment)
www.yardartsF.com

Zonal
568 Hayes
San Francisco, CA 94102   **(415) 255-9307**
Open daily, 11:00 a.m.–6:00 p.m

WASHINGTON, D.C.

Capitol Coin & Stamp Co.
1701 L Street NW
Washington, DC 20036   **(202) 296-0400**
Monday–Saturday, 10:00 a.m.–6:00 p.m.

Georgetown
Flea Market at U Street
1345 U Street NW   **(202) 223-0289**
Saturdays & Sundays, 9:00 a.m.–5:00 p.m.
Admission: Free

Georgetown Flea Market (The original!)
Wisconsin Avenue
between S and T Streets   **(202) 223-0289**
Sundays, March–December, 9:00 a.m.–5:00 p.m.
Admission: Free

Georgia Avenue Thrift Store
6106 Georgia Avenue NW
Washington, DC 20011   **(202) 291-4013**
Monday–Saturday, 9:00 a.m.–9:00 p.m.
Sunday, 11:00 a.m.–7:00 p.m.

Dear Junkers—

Hope you enjoyed Big City Junk! If you have any questions or comments, please visit my website www.carterjunk.com. It's a work in progress, but it will fill you in on my other junk books, any trips I will be making to your part of the world, Carter Junk to buy, a junker's billboard of junking hot spots, plus a lot more! You can email me at carterjunk@hotmail.com or write me at Carter Junk, P.O. Box 718, Millerton, N.Y. 12546.

Junkfully yours,
Mary Randolph Carter
(you can call me "Carter!")

INDEX